Protecting Our Most Valuable Asset

Protecting Our Most Valuable Asset

E. Scott Dunlap

© E. Scott Dunlap, 2017
All rights reserved

ISBN-13: 9781544624211
ISBN-10: 1544624212
Library of Congress Control Number: 2017903928
CreateSpace Independent Publishing Platform
North Charleston, South Carolina

To Leslie for providing me with unwavering support in crossing the country in pursuit of a career I have loved.

To the workers who are getting the job done every day to keep our nation moving.

To the industry leaders who are doing their best each day to provide a safe environment for our workers.

Disclosure: The context, organization, characters, location, and events of material contained within the short story are purely creations of fiction and do not reference or represent actual events.

Contents

Preface · xi
Introduction · xv

Our Most Valuable Asset: A Short Story · · · · · · · · · · · · · · · · · · · 1
   Finding a Job · 3
   On the Course · 6
   The Interview · 10
   A Job Offer · 14
   Visiting the Past · 17
   Lunch · 20
   First Day · 23
   New-Hire Assignments · 27
   Coworker Reflections · 31
   Family · 35
   Engagement · 38
   Skeet · 41
   It Happened · 46
   Gathering the Troops · 52
   Coping · 57
   The Investigation · 61
   The Inspection · 69
   The Settlement · 81

Rebounding · · · 92
Staffing Up · · · 99
Leading the Way · · · 104

Seven Principles to Protect Our Most Valuable Asset · · · 107
    Principle One: Safety Makes Business Sense · · · 109
    Principle Two: Comply · · · 116
    Principle Three: Teach Them · · · 120
    Principle Four: Engage Them · · · 128
    Principle Five: Lead Them · · · 134
    Principle Six: Find It and Fix It · · · 149
    Principle Seven: Measure It · · · 154
    Applying the Seven Principles · · · 165

Charting Your Course · · · 167
    References · · · 173
    Additional Resources · · · 177
    Acknowledgments · · · 179
    About the Author · · · 181

Preface

I grew up in the coal fields of southern West Virginia. Due to the lack of professional sports in our state, we had to look to the north in Pennsylvania or to the west in Ohio to follow televised sports on Saturday or Sunday afternoons. The lack of professional sports also meant that West Virginia University football was a big deal. The state has followed the travails and triumphs of the Mountaineers as the years have rolled by.

In the late-night hours of Monday, January 2, 2006, the Mountaineers were deep in the fourth quarter of the Sugar Bowl. They had opened up the game to an astounding 28–0 lead, but their opponent, the Georgia Bulldogs, had rallied with twenty-eight points; West Virginia had also scored ten more points. With 5:22 left to go in the fourth quarter, the Bulldogs hit a forty-three-yard touchdown pass and a subsequent extra point to bring them within three points. The heart of every West Virginian was nearly in arrest.

After the kickoff return, West Virginia began their march back down the field from their own twenty-two-yard line with 5:06 remaining. A lot of things can happen in five minutes and six seconds with only a three-point lead. West Virginia earned two first downs and was later met with a third down and eleven yards on their own forty-seven yard line after being tackled in the backfield for a loss of yardage. The Mountaineers advanced the ball to the Georgia forty-eight-yard line but were brought down six yards short of a first down. One minute and forty-five seconds remained on the clock. Following a time-out, the Mountaineers came out on the field to punt. After the snap, the West Virginia punter held the ball on his thirty-eight-yard line. He faked the punt and rushed forward to open field. He had to get to the Georgia forty-two-yard line. Red shirts converged on him, but he slid safely across the Georgia thirty-nine-yard line for a first down. It was a classic play. It was first down for West Virginia with 1:38 on the clock, and the game was sealed. Spirits in the state soared. West Virginia was bringing home a bowl victory—the first in eight years.

The next morning, the celebration was quickly dampened as headlines reading "Mountaineers Win Sugar Bowl" were overshadowed by others reading "13 Feared Dead in Sago, West Virginia, Coal Mine Explosion." In the blink of an eye, what should have been a time of jubilation for the state turned into a period of mourning the loss of life as twelve miners were later found dead. Only one had survived.

The nation's attention was drawn to the West Virginia coal fields and the hazards involved in removing coal from under the earth's surface. This work has gone on for generations. My father was a coal miner, as his father had been before him. I grew up knowing the dangers of black lung, roof falls, and methane in our coal mines. This is the reality of the thousands of miners who enter the earth and crawl under the surface of West Virginia and other states across the nation. They do their work with a quiet dignity so that we are able to have light when we flip a switch in our homes.

The lives lost in the Sago mine disaster were a tragedy for family, friends, and the local community. An even greater tragedy is that thousands of other Americans lose their lives each year across numerous industrial sectors while doing the work that must be done to keep our nation moving. These deaths are compounded by the hundreds of thousands of other workers who are injured each year, a large portion of whose injuries are permanently disabling. Yet nothing compares to the tragic fact that these injuries and deaths are preventable, and most are well within our scope of control. According to the Bureau of Labor Statistics, we have been successful in reducing our fatalities in the United States by only 1 or

2 percent each year over the past measured decade. Though some may suggest such a reduction is positive, we are capable of much better. A great deal of opportunity exists for us to more fully integrate workplace safety into our organizational operations.

As an industry leader, you are faced with an extremely complex job. Strengthening the bottom line is the goal of every industry leader. Globalization, rising domestic-labor costs, and harnessing evolving technology have made return on shareholder investment an increasing challenge. As an industry leader, you must rise to this challenge by enhancing the performance of your organization to ensure a competitive position in today's marketplace.

We have warmed up to quality principles and are now transitioning to concepts of lean manufacturing. But there remains one barrier to high organizational performance. It is our dirty little secret of the astounding loss that consistently occurs each year due to events such as the Sago mine disaster. At our current rate of incidents, US business loses as much as $200 billion per year in costs associated with workplace injuries (National Safety Council, 2013; OSHA, accessed April 24, 2017). This cycle of fundamental loss that occurs each year is destined to continue with little improvement unless we make systemic change.

Losses can be greatly reduced if industry leaders gain a greater understanding of ways to protect our most valuable asset: our workers. Such efforts are not simply a cost of doing business but are critical in enhancing the growth of business. US business is in need of an awakening regarding the status quo of loss. The very lives of our workers and the viability of our businesses depend on it.

E. Scott Dunlap
Richmond, Kentucky

Introduction

In the mid-through-late 1900s, W. Edwards Deming challenged industry leaders to consider quality principles. He identified ways in which production could occur not only in volume, but also to a great degree of quality. His quality model is what this book seeks to build upon. One concept that Deming introduced was the need to eliminate waste in the production process. Such waste could include parts damaged in production or time taken to correct errors. Here, I introduce a series of seven principles that address the issue of business loss from a human perspective.

The word *waste* brings to mind things that must be discarded. Another kind of waste is the significant loss of money and employee quality of life that occurs each year in our economy due to fundamental safety issues for our most valuable asset: our workers. According to the Bureau of Labor Statistics (2016a), 49,515 workers died in US workplaces in the last measurable decade (2006–2015)—about ninety-five workers dying on the job each week. In 2015, 1.1 million workers experienced injuries that required them to stay at home for at least one full day to recover (Bureau of Labor Statistics, 2016b). The true numbers of fatalities and injuries in the workplace may actually be much larger since many businesses are not required to report data to the federal government (such as injuries and deaths that occur on family farms and in other small businesses).

Such loss is preventable. We live in an age when our understanding of organizational exposure to workplace-safety risk is comprehensive. We know how to prevent loss that occurs through worker injuries, fatalities, and property damage. Yet a paradox exists: these losses continue at an unnecessarily high rate. The principles I present in this book will help you as an industry leader to implement measures that can increase the quality and productivity of your organization by protecting your workers.

My intention with this book is to take us to a new level of quality management. The principles are designed to improve quality in our work environments—not only of products and services, but also of the quality of life of our workers, which impacts production and performance.

We will explore areas with which industry leaders must become familiar in order to make the most effective organizational decisions. The seven principles here can help you (and any safety professionals you employ) to provide a work environment that encourages greater employee engagement and morale, better compliance with laws, increased productivity, and significant return on investment. Each organization may apply the principles differently according to its culture, safety staffing, and worker and management acceptance of the material. Similarly to Deming's initial work (1950), applying these principles can reduce costs, increase production, and increase quality of products and services and the lives of our workers.

First, I present a short story to illustrate possible successes and failures as outcomes of the principles. It will help you to identify your own organization's potential workplace-safety issues. I then offer a detailed description of each principle and discuss how each can be applied.

You can use this book as a discussion-group tool. The "Charting Your Course" section includes discussion questions that can help you begin your path forward or make course corrections in your current journey.

The material I present may feel overwhelming at first. Or, you may think, *We are already doing all of this stuff.* To address these possibilities, I issue two challenges:

CHALLENGE ONE: TAKE ONE BITE AT A TIME

If you feel overwhelmed by the prospect of what needs to be done in your organization, take heart, as you are not alone. You do not need to address all of the principles at once. Individually or with your leadership team, prioritize the principles according to which offer the most impact and then walk through implementation, taking one bite at a time. The principles are scalable and flexible, allowing you to make meaning of them and apply them to fit the needs of your organization.

CHALLENGE TWO: REFLECT DEEPLY

Let's say you feel that you're already doing everything I recommend. In this case, I challenge you to reflect deeply on *how well* your organization is doing it. For example, your organization might offer a great deal of worker-safety training according to the principle "Teach Them." But if you reflect deeply on your training processes and methodologies, you may identify much opportunity for improvement. You might find that though you have checked the box on the legal requirement to conduct safety training, your company can benefit by increasing the level of learning among workers and management.

Protecting Our Most Valuable Asset

The greatest asset of America today is not its fertile fields, its rich ores, its completely equipped factories, or its millions in currency. The greatest asset in America is the American people. The greatest possible field for economy is not in saving materials but in promoting the safety of our people. The future of the safety movement is not so much dependent upon the invention of safety devices as on the improvement of methods of educating people to the ideal of caution and safety.
  —Walter Dill Scott, a former president of Northwestern University

■ ■ ■

(a) Each employer—
   (1) shall furnish to each of his [her] employees employment and a place of employment which are free from recognized hazards that are causing or are likely to cause death or serious physical harm to his [her] employees;
   (2) shall comply with occupational safety and health standards promulgated under this Act.
(b) Each employee shall comply with occupational safety and health standards and all rules, regulations, and orders issued pursuant to this Act which are applicable to his [her] own actions and conduct.
   —OSHA General Duty Clause from the Williams-Steiger Occupational Safety and Health Act of 1970

■ ■ ■

As the effectiveness of safety and health management systems improve, it is logical to expect that the frequency and severity of occupational injuries and illnesses will be reduced.
  —Fred Manuele, *Advanced Safety Management*

Our Most Valuable Asset:
A Short Story

Finding a Job

Trees were in their height of displaying a dazzling array of colors as fall descended upon Sanford, Illinois, a quiet but growing bedroom community of Champaign. The University of Illinois was well into the first semester of the year, and incoming freshmen were struggling to find a rhythm in their new world.

Billy Ellis had been a U of I fan since birth. It was not a choice he had made; it was part of his DNA. As a freshman majoring in secondary education, Billy was now a third-generation Illini gracing the halls of this prestigious institution. He was also following in the footsteps of his parents by pursuing a career in teaching—but it was not simply something he had inherited; neither had his parents forced it upon him. Billy had a true love of math and saw how it was woven throughout the fabric of our lives. He wanted to learn everything he could about it and pass a sense of its importance on to those who would come behind him. He believed math to be the language of the universe, and he knew that children should be able to use it as easily as they could play the latest video game on the market.

Billy had been gifted with a family that provided the moral support of all of the saints in the church, but their financial resources paled in comparison. However, as his mother, Ruth, would always say, "Where there is a will, there is a way." And Billy was well equipped in the will department. Teaching had always provided a home and lifestyle of moderate means for the Ellis family. Billy always knew that he would work his way through college as both of his parents had done while living at home with his family in Sanford to save on living expenses. He would find a job to pay the remaining tuition that was not covered by a few academic scholarships he had garnered.

Early in the semester, Billy had the good fortune to establish an energetic relationship with his academic advisor, Dr. Stewart Fischer. Dr. Fischer was a stocky gentleman with a presence that filled any room he was in. Fueled by a twenty-ounce injection from Starbucks, Dr. Fischer hit the ground running early each morning. He was the first to enter the office and the last to leave. He loved his job, and he loved his students. He began his day at 6:00 a.m. so he could complete most of his daily administrative tasks before morning classes.

Billy made an appointment to meet with Dr. Fischer at 7:00 a.m. on an October morning. He would have to get up early, because although his first class did not start until 10:00 a.m., it was prime time for Dr. Fischer.

Billy entered Dr. Fischer's immaculately organized office a few minutes early. Dr. Fischer said, "Come on in, Billy! It's great to see you this morning. How are things going?" He motioned for Billy to sit at a round table in the corner, which was his equalizer. He did not want his students to feel they were being lorded over by a professor behind an ominous desk.

Billy replied, "Classes are going great. I wish they were all math classes." He could hear the angelic voice of Alison Krauss singing softly from the radio hidden between rows of books on a shelf.

"Well, you have to take the bad along with the good. Just wait until you get into graduate school. All of your classes there will be the good stuff. You'll be able to focus solely on your area of interest. But that's a long way down the road. Keep focused on the goal of completing your degree, and you'll be fine."

"I know your time is valuable, Dr. Fischer, so I'll get straight to the point. I've mentioned before that I need to take advantage of anything I can to pay for my tuition. I'm able to cover things right now with a few scholarships, a student loan, and my job at the mall. My job is great, because my work schedule fits well around my classes and leaves me enough time to study. The downside is that I don't have enough hours or pay increases to shed student loans."

Dr. Fischer nodded thoughtfully, with his treasure from Starbucks safely secured between his hands.

"Knowing what I can expect to make as a teacher when I finish school, I don't want to be saddled with a bunch of student loan debt."

Dr. Fischer said, "Good thinking. There aren't too many freshmen thinking that far ahead."

"Thanks. I wonder if you might have any ideas about where I could get a better job."

Dr. Fischer leaned back in his chair, thinking deeply as if in another dimension. Coming back to earth, he said, "I play in a weekly fall golf league with a man named Guy Henry. He runs a place called Axeon Logistics over in Sanford. They employ a couple of hundred people. He was talking during our last round of golf about their ramp-up for the holiday season."

"It would be great to work close to home! That way, I would only have to come into town for school. I would be open to doing anything as long as it doesn't interfere with my classes."

"I'll see him Thursday evening. I'll ask if they have anything that might work for you."

"Thanks, Dr. Fischer. I'll try not to get my hopes up. I'll check in with you again on Friday."

On the Course

Axeon Logistics was nestled on the north edge of Sanford. The town had once been a small, isolated community of two thousand residents. For many years, it had enjoyed the blended cultures of corn farming and academia. The majority of its residents were either blue-collar workers associated with local farms or teachers at the University of Illinois. They had enjoyed all of the quaint amenities of small-town life. Its worst type of crime was the annual theft of the high-school mascot statue by the rival Hillsboro High School football team.

The secret of Sanford had somehow been discovered in the mid-1990s, and the town soon tripled in population, with young professionals working in Champaign seeking a quieter refuge where they could start their new families. The thirty-minute commute to Champaign bothered none of Sanford's residents.

Axeon Logistics was not part of the agricultural or academic components of Sanford culture, but it quickly became a fixture in the community. Axeon had been founded in the late eighties as a distributor of home electronic products—things that people simply liked to buy for convenience and entertainment. Axeon had sensed a growing market and mounted its surf board to catch the financial wave. It wholesaled to merchants in Central Illinois and soon grew to cover a tristate area that included Indiana and Kentucky. Axeon was strategically located near the intersections of Interstates 57, 72, and 74 in Champaign, which provided shipping routes in every direction.

Then, production rates and profit margins had dropped steadily through the nineties and into the millennium due to slack management, dealing Axeon two mediocre fiscal-year performances. The company had previously considered itself impervious to the financial woes that affected other industries because of its continued sales volume. However, its owners started to feel differently as commerce went to the Internet. Axeon had been an old-school, low-tech operation, and they saw a need for new growth that their current management team was ill-equipped to provide.

Enter Guy Henry. He was brought in to clean house. With an MBA from Duke, he had been recruited from a national retail organization where he had made world-class advancements in supply chain development. He had grown weary of big-corporate life and looked forward to finishing his working years outside the mainstream rat race and found his home at Axeon Logistics and the cornfields of the Midwest.

Guy towered over most others. He capitalized on that by rarely sitting down at management-team meetings. At his first Axeon meeting, he told his managers and supervisors that fewer than half of them would still be there in a year. They laughed and mocked Guy in private afterward, but his prophecy came true. Of six managers and twenty supervisors at that meeting, only two managers and eight supervisors remained by its first anniversary. Guy displayed little tolerance for poor performance and favored those who were innovative. He fired those who would not quit. And he had the full support of the company owners. The smell of money was in the air, and they knew Guy would lead the way to it.

Guy's one outlet was golf. He had picked the game up later in life but pursued it with the same aggression and passion he used to build his business. His frame and build allowed him to drive the ball a clean three hundred yards. He could get it to go another twenty or thirty if he had a bad day at work.

When Dr. Fischer saw him approach the first tee on this week's round, it was clear what kind of day it had been for Guy. So, Dr. Fischer immediately began to question the idea of exploring the potential of a position at Axeon for Billy. Guy pulled a driver from his bag that was battened down tightly against the back of the golf cart. His hands enveloped the club's grip as he wrenched his fists back and forth around the shaft. The beauty of the early fall evening was not enough to release the pressure that had built within him over the course of what must have been a disastrous day. The only cure was allowing every muscle to release into ripping the small white ball as far as he could send it. Dr. Fischer was relieved when the drive landed safely in the center of the fairway and a slight grin worked its way across Guy's face.

Dr. Fischer also cringed as he wondered whose face Guy had seen on the golf ball moments before crushing it down the fairway. This was a man who could hold a grudge, if only through a short round of golf.

After Guy folded himself into the cart next to Dr. Fischer, they began humming down the path toward their next stage of battle. As usual, the evening opened with perfunctory small talk. "So, Doc, how was your day in the musty halls of academia? I hear you got waxed this weekend in football." A Duke Blue Devil at heart, Guy felt no allegiance to the Illini. He was deep in enemy territory.

"Same old thing. Just trying to mold the minds of America's young men and women."

"And I'm sure you're doing a fine job."

"How was your day?" Dr. Fischer explored tentatively.

"Well, to start with, our quarter-end numbers showed only a fraction of the improvement we'd projected. Our cost per unit is improving sluggishly where it should be dropping like a rock. We have so much low-hanging fruit to pick that a first-year business student could turn the place around. The managers that I have left are barely a notch stronger than the employees on the warehouse floor. My people are content—content with mediocrity and with the way things have been for years. We are getting ready for the holiday season, and I can only imagine what a nightmare that is going to be. But I guess that might have been a little more than you wanted to hear."

"Not at all. I'm always willing to offer a listening ear. It must be frustrating."

"You're darn straight, it's frustrating. I need to increase my warehouse-employee count by five percent over the next week to handle the orders coming in when I can't even get the employees I have to work a solid shift."

"It's funny you mention that. I have a freshman student who needs a job."

"Great. All I need is some fraternity-pledging, slacker Illini working for me. I'm a director of operations, not a babysitter."

"I understand your reservations, Guy. But this young man doesn't live on campus. He lives at home, right in Sanford to save education costs. He's paying his own tuition with a couple of small academic scholarships and a loan. He's working at the mall now but is looking for better pay so he can graduate with less debt."

"At least he doesn't sound like a complete deadbeat." Guy sighed.

"I don't vouch for just anybody. I believe this young man is a hard worker." Dr. Fischer brought the cart to a smooth stop near his ball, which was at least eighty yards short of Guy's.

"Maybe I'll give him a shot. Here's my card. Tell him to give me a call tomorrow. I have to get moving on staffing."

Dr. Fischer pocketed the card.

The Interview

Billy held the business card in his hand as he looked through his car window at Axeon Logistics. His call to Guy Henry on Friday had lasted less than two minutes. He had hoped the call would be more of a phone interview, but apparently, Guy was a busy man. There had been no ice breaking or small talk, just the setting of an appointment graciously doled out by a captain of industry. Any hopes that Billy's apprehension would calm had quickly vanished into thin air as he'd clicked off his cell phone. The appointment had been for 10:00 a.m.—conflicting with one of Billy's chemistry labs. Guy had never inquired about Billy's class schedule, and he had had no time to discuss it before he realized the phone call was over.

He eased out of his car after checking his appearance one last time in the rearview mirror. Fortunately, his hair had cooperated nicely. Though his mom had suggested the outfit, he felt comfortable in his clothes—khakis and a white button-down shirt and blue tie. He made his way up the few steps to the front door, taking one last deep breath before pulling on the handle.

He had no particular expectations about the job, because this was his first exposure to a real one. He had worked since mowing his first yard for five bucks at the age of twelve, moving on to the teen career path of fast-food and mall retail stores. Billy knew he was getting ready to step onto a different plane of existence. People working at Axeon were not simply making money for the weekend or to pay for college like his previous coworkers. They were paying down mortgages, making car payments, and putting food on the table.

"May I help you?" asked a bland voice from behind a raised counter.

Billy stepped toward the voice to find a young receptionist looking impatiently in his direction. He must have interrupted her reading the novel spread out on the desk in front of her. "Yes, please. I'm here for a ten o'clock appointment with Mr. Henry."

"Have a seat," she said, punching numbers into her massive phone from memory.

Billy turned to find a place to sit and noticed two chairs in the far corner of glass walls extending two stories to the vaulted ceiling above. As he approached the corner he noticed that the chairs were worn and stained, so he decided to stand.

At 10:20 a.m., the receptionist called for Billy to follow her through the only other door in the lobby, of windowless wood stained the color of coffee with a little too much cream in it. Billy was surprised to be immediately plunged into a world of dark gray concrete with pallet racking a short distance away that towered forty feet high and was lit with halogens in the oddest shade of yellow. He was on another planet.

The receptionist kept them between yellow pedestrian lines painted over the gray concrete. They made a quick right and traveled along the side of a cinder-block wall. As they made the turn, Billy was met with an area of dock doors that stretched away from him to his left as far as he could see. The building had not looked quite so large from the outside.

They soon ducked into a hallway that brought Billy back to earth. The receptionist's heels clicked across black-and-white tiles. Cleanly painted walls were covered with framed posters showing the most beautiful landscapes. Each print was captioned with a bit of wisdom that was sure to make you a better person than you were before you had read it.

The receptionist clicked to a stop before the door at the end of the hall. She rapped on it with three quick pecks of her knuckles. "Come in," a muffled voice barely made it through the door. The receptionist turned abruptly, leaving Billy standing alone in front of the door, her duty done. "Come in," crept through the door once more as Billy watched the receptionist walk away. His heart began to pound, and he could hear a soft thumping in his ears. He reached slowly for the door knob and gently turned it. The door drifted open.

The wall directly across from him was glass from floor to ceiling. He could see tractors and trailers being moved rapidly outside. Guy Henry sat off to his right, behind an expansive desk with piles of papers strewn about. Billy felt as though he was an intruder in the private sanctuary of Guy Henry and even more unnerved by the lack of acknowledgment by the man, who was glued to a computer screen, typing furiously. "Have a seat," Guy finally said.

Billy quietly closed the door. Though the office was large, there was only a lone chair directly across the desk from Guy: facing the throne. "Thank you," Billy said as he scooted the chair back a couple of inches and sat down.

Guy finished typing for a moment and leaned back in his chair, interlacing his fingers behind his head. He stared momentarily at Billy as if to size up his prey. Billy had a brief memory of being called to the principal's office when he was in the fifth grade. He had been accused of a crime he did not commit, but Principal Eldridge had grilled him for what had seemed an eternity.

Billy's bowels began to rumble as a cold sweat broke out over his body.

"Why should I hire you, Billy Ellis?" The question sent the message that the interview would last about as long as the phone call the previous Friday.

Billy knew he had to get to the point quickly. "I work hard, I learn fast, and I will be here every day. I am—"

"Dr. Fischer has put his neck on the line for you. Why should I trust what he has to say?"

"I've known Dr. Fischer since starting at the university. We hit it off pretty well. He has seen my work in school, and I think he knows I will put that same energy into my job. He and I—"

"What work do you do now?"

"I work at the mall, stocking in a department store. I work there twenty hours each week while going to school full time. I am busy, but—"

"The job I have here is full time, forty hours a week, and maybe some weekend work as we get a little closer to Christmas. Can you handle that?"

"Yes, sir. I'm sure I—"

"Good enough. You might get a call from us within the next few days. Can you find your way back out?"

While rising from his seat and extending his right hand for a departing shake, Billy said, "Yes, I believe so. Thank you for your time."

Guy gripped Billy's hand around the fingers rather than all the way into the palm. Billy never knew he could experience so much pain while keeping a smile on his face.

Billy turned to leave the office as the keyboard started chattering behind him.

A Job Offer

The call came two days later. Billy would become an Axeon Logistics employee the following Friday. Orientation would be at 1:00 p.m. sharp. "If you are going to be late, don't bother coming," the receptionist said as she hung up.

Billy felt an excitement that he had not felt since opening his University of Illinois acceptance letter the previous year. He had a real full-time job. He would work second shift, and for that, Billy was very happy, because he would not have to change his class schedule, and he could sleep on a somewhat normal schedule. His bliss finally came crashing down when he realized that he would not be able to give a two-week notice at the mall. But sacrifices had to be made. Axeon Logistics was Billy's train, and it was pulling out of the station fast. He would be on board.

"Are you sure this is what you want to do?" asked Billy's father, Sam. They were seated around their kitchen table, eating dinner. For the Ellis family, meals were more of an event than simply for eating. Dinners such as these had become less frequent as Billy had started college, but the family took the advantage of having them every day they could. Dinner was a chance to touch base on what was going on in everyone's busy lives.

"Definitely. I'll be able to work more hours and make more money per hour. I'll be able to pay my tuition easily and maybe even pay back my student loans from this year, before I graduate."

"I know," Sam said uneasily. "I'm happy for you. I just wish your mom and I could help out more with money."

While slicing into his grilled chicken breast, Billy said, "Don't worry, Dad, I'll have plenty of time for class and study during the mornings and weekends. It'll be okay."

"Make sure you keep your schoolwork as your priority. Axeon is not the goal. Teaching is."

Ruth jumped in. "He'll be okay, Sam. He knows what he's doing. We raised him right. And if he gets too far off the path, I have that stick in the pantry to get him back on the straight and narrow." Billy smiled, knowing his mother would not hurt a flea.

"That's right, Dad. Spare the rod, spoil the teaching career."

Forks and knives clicked against plates as a rare moment of silence descended on the table, each bite savored as if it were at the family's last meal. Sam resurrected the conversation. "So, what do you know about the company?"

"They have been in a little trouble, but the new manager, Guy Henry, was brought in to straighten things out. He's been doing a great job, from what I hear."

"And Dr. Fischer recommended them?" Ruth asked.

"He didn't really recommend them. I met with Dr. Fischer last week and told him I needed a better job, hoping that he might have some ideas of where I could look. He happens to play golf with Mr. Henry. But I can tell you that golf is the only thing that Dr. Fischer and Mr. Henry have in common."

"What do you mean?" Ruth asked, scooping a second serving of steamed vegetables onto her plate.

"Nothing, really. It's just that Mr. Henry seemed busy, and I felt like I was keeping him from his work during the interview. I thought we would have more time to talk, but I'm sure he's an important man and had things on his mind."

Sam asked, "Do you think that is a sign of things to come? That is a big place, and there are a lot of things you'll need to know before they put you out on the floor working."

"I'm sure I'll go through enough training. We didn't discuss it, but I'm sure things will go smoothly with all of the work Mr. Henry has done to improve the business."

"How can you be sure?"

"Well, I can't be sure. But they can't be doing as well as they are without having a good program in place to train people. I'll be fine."

Sam wiped his mouth and dropped the napkin on his clean plate. "Okay, we'll see how things are going after your first week. Now for more important business. Where is the pineapple upside-down cake?"

Visiting the Past

Billy's supervisor at the mall was not happy with his short notice of departure, but she understood. Turnover at the mall in a college town was as natural as breathing. She knew she was losing a great employee and that it had always been just a matter of time until he found something that paid a little better. The mall could only offer so much to maintain a profit and its real estate in the high-rent district. Salaries were tightly managed.

Billy thought back to his first week at the mall as he finished his last shift. Ms. Ferguson had spent so much time with him to make sure he knew every aspect of his job. "We all serve the customer," she would say. "Whether you work stocking merchandise or directly with customers in sales, everyone has a stake in the experience customers have when they come into our store."

Ms. Ferguson had focused a great deal on housekeeping. Billy was a stocker, so this had been a large part of his position. Department sales associates were responsible for making sure their areas always looked pristine, and Billy was there to support them. New merchandise was always delivered to departments late in the day and put away by early the next morning to minimize customer exposure to boxes and piled merchandise. Everyone was responsible to ensure the store was neat, clean, and orderly throughout their shifts. A busy day with high storewide sales was no exception. Though shoppers rolled through with the force of a hurricane, Ms. Ferguson demanded that the store always look as if it had just opened its doors.

A closing interview was a part of the process whenever an employee left the company. Billy arrived in Ms. Ferguson's office on schedule. It was decorated with personal touches everywhere. Though she had never married, she had photos of brothers, sisters, nephews, and nieces on every available surface. It gave Billy the sense of walking into a living room. Instead of a meeting table, she had four wing chairs positioned around a small glass coffee table. This was where Billy and Ms. Ferguson sat for the closing interview.

"We're going to miss you, Billy," Ms. Ferguson began while handing him a cold Dr Pepper. She knew it was his soft drink of choice. "You have been a great asset to our team. I wish there was something I could do to keep you here."

"I wish I could stay. You've been very helpful with me on my schedule, but unfortunately, it all comes down to money. I never thought it would be a driving force in my life, but I don't look forward to having a large student loan debt hanging over my head when I finish school."

"Axeon is getting a great young man, and I am sure they will soon appreciate what you have to offer them. You've definitely improved the way product flows through the store. Your ideas have helped us to streamline the time it takes to get merchandise on the racks once it lands on our dock. I'm also certain that the sales associates appreciate it because it has helped them leave a lot earlier after closing than before."

"I was a little afraid to bring ideas up, because I didn't want you to think I was being critical. The way you responded made me feel really good about myself. It made me feel like I was part of a team and not just a lowly stocker in such a big company."

"Billy, I'm a strong believer that the best ideas in any workplace come from the people doing the work. Management may often think that because they have the college degrees and the years of work experience, they have all of the answers. It simply isn't so. In a short few weeks, you were able to learn a system and detect ways to make it better. It made our employees happier and saved our store a lot of money in the process."

"I really like being involved in things."

"Your work on our safety committee was also very much appreciated. Your ideas about controlling loss through our processes also made a good fit for you in our safety efforts. The training session you came up with on proper lifting technique has helped us reduce our back injuries by twenty percent. Make sure you do the same thing once you get settled into Axeon. I am certain they will want to hear any ideas that you have."

Lunch

"I have to go to work after class," Billy told Katrina as they walked across campus in search of something to eat. Hunting and gathering now amounted to cruising the eating establishments that campus had to offer.

Billy and Katrina had known each other since her family had moved to town during her junior year in high school. This had made her bitter toward her parents because she had been forced to leave all of her close friends behind and start fresh once again. Her father had promised that the previous relocation was to be their last, but then came the movers, and they were off to the Midwest.

The issue had been softened a little once she'd met Billy in chemistry class when they became lab partners, but the relationship soon went much deeper. They were an unlikely pair, with her in the most popular brands from head to toe and him wearing what was on sale at Walmart. He liked that she did not care about that kind of thing. She was just the lucky recipient of a little family money.

"What time does your shift start?" asked Katrina.

"Right after lunch at one o'clock. This shift couldn't be any better." He loved to mention "going to work" and "working a shift." His game had been officially elevated. "Kat, it's like the clouds have parted and opened up a whole new dream of what life will be like after college. I've been dying to find a job like this. I always thought that I would have student loan debt to fight on a teacher's salary, but now I'll be able to make a fresh start. Maybe even be able to buy a house before I'm twenty-five. Who knows?"

"Don't get ahead of yourself. I'm happy for you, but I hope it won't wear you out. It sounds like a lot to take on."

"I'll be okay."

They stepped into the food court and settled on sub sandwiches—Italian on white for him and turkey breast on wheat for her. Though she had the build of a track star, Kat worked diligently to keep her body in as good a shape as her mind.

They settled into their customary table near a stone fireplace with its gas flame. "I'm starting at ten dollars per hour," Billy continued. "That is a nice bump from what I was making at the mall. So, I'll be bringing home around fifteen thousand each year. Dad helped me design a budget. It's not like I'll be rich, but he wants to make sure I manage it well."

"That's good, because I don't want to see you blowing it on big screens and other gizmos."

"Not hardly. But I might treat myself to a new laptop. Our desktop at home is getting a little age on it, and it would be nice to have something to carry to campus with me. That would help me even more to mesh studying and projects with my work schedule. I hear we get some kind of discount on merchandise we distribute. I'll have to check that out. Maybe that will be an avenue for Christmas shopping for me. Avoiding the mall and doing it from work wouldn't be a bad thing."

"What does your first day at work look like?"

"I'm not sure. I haven't been told much other than to be there at 1:00 p.m. today. I'm guessing today will be a light day— probably an orientation class, fill out paperwork, and get a tour of the facility. My first day at the mall went a little like that."

Kat chewed on a bite of her sub. Then she got an odd feeling. "You mean to say they haven't told you what to expect?"

"No. But I'm sure it'll be okay. It's a busy place, and they're having a lot of problems getting production to where it needs to be. I'm probably the last thing on their minds."

"What kind of problems?"

"They haven't been as profitable as they should be, and Mr. Henry was brought in to straighten things out. He has made a lot of changes, but it sounds like a lot more need to be made. He has had a hard time finding good workers, and that is what opened the door for me. The timing is perfect. I think I can have a lot of good input. I like looking at problems and figuring out how to make things work better. Ms. Ferguson at the mall encouraged me to speak up when I get used to the job. She liked what I did in stocking and thinks I should step forward with ideas at Axeon."

"That is if they want to hear what you have to say. Some managers think they have all of the answers."

"I know what you mean. I'll have to feel things out once I start working."

After dumping their trays, they stepped out into a cool afternoon. Campus was alive with every color that fall had to offer. Maybe it was a good sign for a good first day on the job.

"Have a great day at work," Kat said.

"Thanks. See you tomorrow." He stood just for a moment to watch as she walked away.

First Day

Billy arrived fifteen minutes early for his shift. He wanted to make a good impression even though he had secured the job. He recognized the receptionist as he entered—the same he had spoken with the day of his interview. She greeted him without making eye contact. "Through the door and to the left. You'll see a set of red double doors. Go through them and take a seat." The web page she was surfing was apparently more important than her conversation with him.

The training room was a collage of mismatched tables and vintage 1970s chairs with worn upholstery. It was an historical landscape of office furniture from days gone by, a landfill of outcasts. Sun-bleached artwork adorned the walls that yearned for a fresh coat of paint. Three other new-hire employees sat in the room, each in different corners, staring at the chipped vinyl-tile floor.

"Hello," Billy said as he entered the room. He was rewarded with only a brief glance and nod of the head by one young man. Billy decided to sit a couple of chairs away from him.

They sat in silence, waiting for their orientation to begin. The receptionist walked into the room twenty minutes late, carrying a stack of papers. She laid them on the desk at the front of the room. Walking over to each person, she handed them a pile of papers. "You need to fill out the I-9, tax form, and benefits-enrollment form. I will give you a few minutes to do that, and I'll be right back."

"Do you have a pen?" asked the young man near Billy as the receptionist neared the door to leave the room. She stopped and dropped her head, shaking it ever so slightly. She turned and went to the table, picking up her new employee roster.

"Shane Evans?"

"That's right."

"Do you plan to show up for work unprepared each day?"

"No. I didn't realize I would need a pen today. No one told me what to bring, so I just showed up."

"That brain in your head is for thinking. You should start making better use of it. I'll be back in a minute with a pen for you. Does anyone else need one?" The other two new hires in the room cautiously raised their hands while Billy quietly pulled a pen out of his pocket.

The receptionist left the room, shaking her head.

"What's her problem?" asked the woman in the back left corner of the room. "I'm old enough to be her mother. And she treats me like that? She needs a little attitude adjustment."

"Witch," said the man in the other corner. "They're all like that. She works up in her nice, clean office while we have to go out there and make things happen. If it wasn't for us, she wouldn't have a job."

Billy attempted a weak defense. "Maybe she's just having a bad day."

Shane said, "She must have been having a bad day when I was here for my interview, too. I bet she has a lot of bad days."

The receptionist returned, and silence blanketed the room. "Here are your pens. Unless anyone needs anything else, I will give you a few minutes to complete your paperwork. I will be out front at my desk if you have any questions." She quickly turned and left.

The woman said, "It's like she's afraid of catching something from us. I don't know what to put on these forms. I haven't filled out anything like this in fifteen years."

Billy offered, "I can probably help you. I just went through this with my job at the mall not too long ago."

The woman got up and moved to a chair next to Billy. "I'm Agnes Rutherford," she said, reaching her hand out.

"Billy Ellis," he replied, shaking her hand. He found her hand to be rough and her grip strong. She was no one to tangle with. He knew he could depend on her. He could tell things like that about people.

"What are you in for?" asked Agnes.

"School bills. I'm a student at the U of I."

"A college boy! Good for you. I barely made it past my high-school diploma. I got married right after that and never looked back."

"What brought you here?" Billy asked.

"My husband left, and I've got two boys at home to raise."

"I'm sorry to hear that."

"Just because he left doesn't mean life has to stop. My boys are strong, and this job will put food on the table. Everything will be all right."

"I'm Harley," said the man in the corner. "Harley Beach."

"Nice to meet you, Harley Beach."

Billy and Agnes took their turns shaking hands. "What brought *you* here?" Agnes asked.

"I run a small crop south of town, and it's been getting tougher each year to make ends meet. I had to do something, and this is it."

"How about you, Shane?" Billy asked, pulling him into the group.

"Just got married."

Agnes said, "Married? Honey, you don't look old enough to have a driver's license."

Shane dropped his head as his face turned a slight shade of red. "I'm nineteen and can take care of myself. I've learned a big lesson. You can make a lot of choices, but the consequences aren't up to you."

Billy and Harley stared at each other with blank looks, but Agnes knew that Shane had meant that a baby was on the way. Slapping his back, she said, "It'll be all right, honey. You just wait and see."

Billy said, "We better get on this paperwork. The ice queen will be back in a few minutes, and we better not let her catch us unprepared for whatever she has next."

They quickly made their way through the forms, helping one another wherever needed.

The receptionist came back as they were signing the last form. "Are we all done?" she asked.

She was rewarded with nods of each head.

"Good. Now each of you will need to go out to your departments. Your supervisors will take over things from there. Wait for a few minutes, and they will be in here to take you where you need to go. Welcome to Axeon." She gathered her papers and made a quick exit.

New-Hire Assignments

Shane and Agnes were the first to go to their positions. Shane had been assigned to work in the Stocking Department, and Agnes would be working in the Order Selecting Department. Harley and Billy sat talking in the room, waiting for their supervisor.

A hefty man with a sweat-stained shirt burst in. "Frank Perry, maintenance manager," he said, reaching his hand out to Harley and Billy for a quick shake. After pulling his hand away, Billy felt a need to wash it. "It's another day in the jungle. Both of you need to follow me. We've got a lot going on right now." Frank turned to leave as quickly as he had come in. Billy and Harley tried to keep up.

They had been assigned to the Maintenance Department. This choice surprised Billy because he had little mechanical aptitude, but he was told he would not need to work on equipment. He would be a maintenance specialist—a glorified title for a laborer or "gopher," as his dad called it. Billy would "go for" whatever the mechanics needed and clean up after them.

Frank addressed the new men. "We have a conveyor down that sends a lot of product to our shipping dock, so it's all hands on deck. Harley, I understand you know your way around a tool box."

"That's right. I've had to keep things running around the farm since I was a kid. There isn't much I can't fix."

"Good to hear. Billy, you just hang close, and we'll let you know if we need something."

"You mean we're heading straight to work right now? What about getting trained on what we're supposed to do?" Billy asked as they hustled through the facility.

"Son, this isn't school, where you get to sit around and read books and talk about things. This is the real world, where you have to jump in with both feet and get the job done. Just remember the letters O-J-T—on-the-job training. You'll learn by doing, making mistakes, and then getting it right. Hopefully, you won't make too many mistakes. Just watch what folks are doing around you, and you'll be fine. If this conveyor stays down, product doesn't get out the door. If product doesn't get out the door, our customers aren't happy. If our customers aren't happy, our boss, Mr. Henry, isn't happy. And if he isn't happy, our world is a very dark place to live in."

They bobbed and weaved through the facility until they arrived at the epicenter of their problem. A piece of merchandise that had not been properly sealed into a tote had fallen out at the worst possible time and place. Instead of the floor, it had landed in a primary drive section of the conveyor, getting caught and causing the conveyor to grind to a stop. The drive motor had continued to run and burned itself out to an agonizing end. These two problems had caused the belt to snap in half under the stress.

Shaking his head, Harley said, "That conveyor belt looks a little ragged around the edges. It looks like it should have been changed out a while ago."

"It was working fine and would have kept going. Order selectors get in too much of a hurry, don't pack loads correctly, and this kind of stuff happens. They don't care what happens to things downstream from them as long as they kick out the work they are supposed to do."

Harley said, "The grain elevator I deliver my corn to over in Plattsburgh has slowdown switches on the conveyors that turn them off if a jam occurs. Maybe we could look at something like that here."

Frank scoffed, "Those things cost money. And money is something we don't have."

"But I thought Axeon has been gaining in profits," Billy said.

Frank said, "We have. There is money for some things, but maintenance isn't one of them. Even though we're doing better, our mission is to cut expenses. Cut, cut, cut. Our budget has to stay flat this year or go lower. Asking for more money isn't an option."

This did not compute for Billy. Even he knew that it cost money to maintain something as small as a car. As the years rolled by and a vehicle aged, certain costs of repair and maintenance would naturally spike once in a while. In the early years, a car only needed a simple oil change, but one day, it would need new brakes or maybe even worse—a new transmission. Regardless, it all cost money. He could only imagine what it cost to maintain a building like the one he was now working in.

"How does Mr. Henry expect you to keep things running if you don't have money to properly repair equipment?" Billy asked.

One of Frank's maintenance technicians was elbow deep into repairing the conveyor. Grinning, the technician said, "Out of the mouths of babes. There are some things you just don't ask around here. And you never question Mr. Henry."

"But I—"

"It doesn't matter what you meant. You just do your job the best you can and then go home when the day is over," said the technician, Skeet Davis, who was a jaded veteran. The fight in him was long gone.

Frank said, "Skeet, get the conveyor running, and let me worry about the new guy. He'll learn soon enough. How much longer?"

"Give me another fifteen minutes. Hey, Reggie! Hit the power and let me see if we have current!"

Reggie stood up, towering over the group. With a drawn scowl on his face, he shuffled to the main electrical panel and flipped a breaker switch to the "on" position.

Billy immediately flinched. "Shouldn't you have that locked out while you're working on it? That's what the electricians at the mall have to do."

"Locked out? You mean I should take the time to turn off the switch and put a padlock on the panel door while I'm working on this?"

Billy said, "That way, you can be sure that you won't get hurt while you're working on the conveyor. If you don't do that but just turn it off, someone could come by while you're not looking and turn it on by mistake. If that happened when you were not expecting it, you could get your arm caught in the conveyor or be electrocuted if you were touching bare wires at the moment."

Skeet chuckled, "Well, folks, it looks like we have us a safety man here. He's going to save all of us. I don't have time for that every time something around here goes down. Besides that, electrical panels are sometimes a long way from where we're working. Maintenance is a tight group of guys, and we watch out for one another. We know who is working on what, and we're all careful. We've been doing this for a long time, kid."

Billy had started to learn. This was one of those times when he needed to keep his mouth closed.

Coworker Reflections

The lunchroom was a poorly lit cinder-block chamber near the back of the facility. A convenient door was located in the rear corner for the smokers to get their fix before going back to work. Billy and Harley found Shane and Agnes at a round table. Billy could tell by the looks on their faces that this was going to be an interesting lunch break.

"So, how's it going so far?" Harley asked no one in particular as he pulled his food out of his Carhartt lunch bag. He neatly spread his sandwich, chips, and dessert before him. Everyone could tell that Harley's wife had had something to do with his meal getting put together.

Shane's eyes were large saucers. "They put me on a stock picker already!"

"What is that?" Agnes asked.

Shane said, "It's a lift like you see at the home-improvement store. You stand on it and drive around on it. When you get to the rack you need to go to, you hit a button, and it raises you off the floor like an elevator. And I'm afraid of heights!"

"Didn't your supervisor ask you about that before he put you on it?" Billy asked.

"No. He just said that he needed someone to run that type of lift, and that was it. He teamed me up with a guy who's been here for a few years and operates the same type of lift. But all he did was run through how everything was supposed to work and then made me follow him around for about thirty minutes. After that, he said I looked like I was doing fine—and I haven't seen him since."

Harley said, "You'll get used to it. Think of it as an adventure. You get to ride around all shift on a piece of motorized equipment while Billy and I have to go around repairing things. You've got it made."

"I heard a lady fell off one last month," Shane said.

"Fell off one? How did she do that?" Billy asked.

"We're supposed to use a harness and lanyard to tie off to the lift before we start moving. That way, if we slip and fall while we are up off the floor, it will catch us. I heard she was in a hurry and forgot to put her harness on or just thought that she wouldn't need it because she was doing a quick job. No one knows for sure. She slipped and fell off the lift while she had it about five feet off of the ground. They say she hit her head and broke a couple of bones."

"That's terrible!" Agnes said.

Billy quietly shook his head as he swallowed a gulp of Dr Pepper. "How old is she?"

"She's my age," Shane replied. Billy now more fully understood Shane's fear. He was thinking that if it could happen to her, then it could happen to him.

Billy tried to console him. "People make mistakes."

"I know, but what if I make the same mistake?"

Billy said, "You won't. Take what happened to her as a learning experience. You now know what can happen if you don't tie off with your harness and lanyard. Go through a mental checklist each time you get ready to start moving. Make sure your harness is snug and your lanyard is attached to the equipment. You'll be okay."

Agnes said, "Of course you will. What happened to that woman was terrible, but we can learn from things like that."

"How has your work been going, Agnes?" Harley asked as he wiped his mouth with his shirt sleeve.

"I think I'll like it. It's busy, and the time goes by fast."

"What kind of things are you doing?" Billy asked.

"We receive orders transmitted to us on a little handheld computer that tells me what I'm supposed to pick for an order. It's been a while since I've had a job outside the home, but I never thought a computer would be telling me what to do."

They all laughed a little, in need of breaking the tension.

Agnes continued, "We just pull things out of what they call 'pick slots.' I put all of the merchandise in plastic totes. Once a tote is full, I put it on a conveyor that takes it to Shipping."

Shane said, "Maybe I could come to work in your area. It sounds like I wouldn't have to worry about falling."

Agnes replied, "That's true. But one thing that bothers me is a few of the workers in my area are wearing wrist braces."

Harley said, "Why? It sounds like a brace would make it harder to do your job."

"I asked one of the ladies that I work with, and she said it was because her hands started hurting after she worked here for a while."

"Did she report her problem to her supervisor?" Billy asked.

"She did, but she was told to try the brace and put ice on it after work."

"Didn't she go see a doctor?" Shane asked.

"No. Her supervisor keeps telling her it will get better. But she has been here for ten months, and she still hurts quite a bit. She's afraid to push things, because she really needs this job and doesn't want to make waves. Her family needs the health insurance."

Billy said, "A coworker of mine at the mall suffered a back injury, and workers' comp took care of his medical bills. I'm sure Axeon has a workers' compensation program and won't penalize her for reporting an injury. Even though they didn't give us a detailed orientation before they sent us out here, one of the papers we signed said we are Axeon's 'most valuable asset,' and we are supposed to report injuries immediately."

"That's right," Harley said.

Agnes said, "I'll talk to her. So, how are things in the Maintenance Department?"

"Well, I'm not afraid of falling like Shane is, but we might get electrocuted," Billy said.

Harley quipped, "You're being a little dramatic, son. It isn't that bad."

Ignoring Harley, Shane asked Billy, "What do you mean?"

"They took us straight out to where a conveyor belt was down. Before working on electrical equipment, you are supposed to turn off the power, close the panel door, and put a padlock on it that only you have the key to. That way, no one can come by and accidentally turn it on while you are working on the damaged equipment."

"I've never heard of that, but it makes good sense to me," Agnes said.

Billy said, "Two maintenance technicians were working on the conveyor, and neither one of them had a lock on the panel. They said it takes too long and that they all just look out for one another."

"Isn't that good enough?" Shane asked.

Billy said, "It's kind of like your harness. You can't always depend on me to be looking out for you and remind you to put it on. You have to take responsibility for your safety and the safety of people working around you. It's good to look out for one another, but we have to take the initiative to protect ourselves."

"I see what you're saying," Shane said.

"It's great to work as a team, but we also have to look at safety as a personal responsibility," Billy said.

Family

"There's the working man!" Sam said as Billy and Kat walked into the backyard. Dinner at the Ellis house tonight was burgers and hot dogs on the grill. They were enjoying one of the last few warm days before packing in the yard gear for the season.

"How are you doing, Kat?" Ruth asked as she stepped in for a tight hug.

"Everything is going fine so far this semester. No big surprises yet."

Ruth turned to Billy. "How about you?" She reached up to hug the neck of her son.

"Not too bad. Work is an adjustment, but other than that, school is going great."

"Give us the scoop on Axeon," Sam said as he powdered the burgers with seasoning. "Is it everything you dreamed it would be?"

"That and more," Billy said with a wry smile.

Ruth said, "That doesn't sound too good. What's going on?"

Billy hesitated long enough for Kat to dig an elbow in his side. "Tell them," she said.

"Tell us what?" Sam turned to them, allowing his work of art to sit idle and cook to perfection.

Billy attempted a weak exit from the topic. "It's nothing."

Kat kept things on course. "Yes, it is. Tell them what it's like."

"It's just different from the mall. Things move a lot faster, but that's to be expected. Axeon is a big place with a lot of big customers. It's just different."

"How is it different?" Ruth asked.

"Tell them about your 'training,'" Kat said, ending with air quotes.

Billy relented. "After we filled out our paperwork, we were sent straight out to work. Instead of taking us through formal training before we started in our departments, they took us out to our work area for on-the-job training."

"Is that as good as going through a formal training program?" Sam asked.

Billy rationalized, "It's just a different way of doing it. They've been very successful since Mr. Henry started managing the facility, so it must work. I'm just not used to it."

Kat said, "On-the-job training is just window dressing for having no training." Billy had been with Kat long enough to know that everyone would hear her opinion whether it was solicited or not. She argued, "Management just puts new employees on a job, expecting them to learn by absorbing things from their environment. What if they absorb the wrong things? What if older employees are not doing things exactly the way they should be?"

Billy said, "Skeet and those guys have been around a long time, Kat. I'm sure they know what they're doing. They do take a few risks, but they seem to get the job done. And that's what counts."

Kat said, "A few risks? It only takes one to seriously hurt or kill someone."

"Don't be melodramatic," Billy said.

Kat said, "I'm not. What happened to all of the things you used to do at the mall? Axeon doesn't even have a safety committee."

Billy said, "Mr. Henry has to make a lot of changes to make sure Axeon becomes and remains profitable. He's under a lot of pressure."

"That's not an excuse for an unsafe work environment," Kat said.

Billy responded, "I'm sure he'll start working on safety once he has production under control."

"Can't he do both at the same time?" Sam asked.

Kat said, "Sure they can. If employees know they're cared for and are in a safe work environment, their performance will be much stronger."

Billy said, "That is true. One of my new friends who started the same day I did works in the Order Selecting Department. She said a lot of her coworkers are wearing braces because of pain they have from doing the same motions day after day with their hands and wrists. I'm sure they would be able to work a lot better if there was a way to lessen their pain."

Kat said, "There is a way. It's called ergonomics. We talked about it the other day in my kinesiology class at school."

"What is ergonomics?" Ruth asked.

"It's how our bodies fit into our environment. One example is what auto manufacturers have done with seats in cars. Years ago, most cars had bench seats that were not very comfortable for long trips."

Sam said, "I remember those days. Driving from here to Myrtle Beach on vacation was painful."

Kat said, "Cars now have form-fitting seats with much more support and comfort. Controls are in easy reach, so the driver doesn't have to stretch to change the temperature or adjust the stereo. The same principles can be applied to workplaces. Think about how much stress Axeon employees' bodies go through every day. Things as simple as stretching, breaks, and job rotation can help. Though these may not be traditional items in a work schedule, they can actually increase production because employees are healthier."

"Can that stuff be done at Axeon?" Sam asked.

Billy replied, "I think so. But Mr. Henry is dealing with so many other problems that it probably won't be at the top his list for a while."

"It sounds like if it were, it might solve some of his other problems," Ruth said.

Billy said, "It would. I think I'll talk to some of my friends and see how we can recommend something."

Engagement

Billy had spoken to Harley, Shane, and Agnes about integrating safety into their departments. They all thought it was a great idea. It would be a win-win because employees would feel better about coming to work, and Axeon would reap higher and more consistent production.

Billy was able to make his safety recommendation to Mr. Henry following a shift meeting one afternoon. "Mr. Henry, can I have a minute of your time?" he asked as Guy was making a quick exit back to his office.

Guy turned in surprise. "Sure, but I only have a minute. I have to be in my office for a conference call."

"Yes, sir, I'll be quick. I have an idea that might help boost production."

That got Guy's attention. "I'm always open to ways to make things move faster. What do you have?"

"We should consider implementing a safety program. We have a lot of employees nursing pain throughout their shifts, and I'm sure that slows them down a lot, not to mention the physical harm it is causing them. Maybe we could look at ways to do our jobs safer."

"I thought you were going to talk about a process change," Guy said as his shoulders slumped slightly.

"Safety will have an impact on processes. Employees will feel more comfortable here, so it will help them mentally. It will also help production, because healthy employees perform at a much higher rate than if they are nursing an injury."

"Do you think I am operating an unsafe facility?"

Billy knew he was now on thin ice. "I don't think it is completely unsafe, but I do think there are things we can do to make it safer."

"Like what?"

"We could have more detailed training to prepare workers to do their jobs, particularly with lift equipment. There are hazards associated with our jobs that we could more safely manage if we were trained before being released to the floor."

"How long would this training take?"

"It depends. If someone is already experienced, the training wouldn't take as long. But if you want someone to operate a lift who never has before, training may take a day or two."

"A day or two! You would expect me to pay for hours of nonproduction?"

"But once they went through training, employees would feel more comfortable doing their work, and they could do it faster."

"Our training is good enough now. New hires are teamed up with experienced workers and learn as they go. That's the way I learned, and I think that's the best way."

Billy could hear the ice beginning to crack beneath him.

"Come back to me when you have a good idea," Guy said as he turned and left.

— — —

"How did it go?" Harley asked as his coworkers settled at their table for lunch.

Billy answered, "You don't want to know"

"What happened?" Shane asked.

"Did he even listen to you?" Agnes asked.

Billy said, "Yeah, he listened to me. He thinks our training is good enough and wasn't concerned about safety."

"I thought the potential production increase might get his attention," Shane said.

"It did for a minute, but he didn't see the connection," Billy said.

Harley said, "How could he not see it? It makes perfect sense. I know I haven't been the poster child for safety on my farm, but us talking has made me think again about how I work out there."

Billy said, "It sounded like what we do here is the way he learned to do things, so he's just doing what he's learned."

"This may not be his only problem," Shane said.

Harley asked, "What else is going on?"

"Some employees are stealing things."

Agnes asked, "Why would they do that? We get a nice employee discount on the merchandise we distribute. I plan on using it to get my kids a new computer for Christmas."

Shane said, "Maybe you guys should ask your friend Skeet. Some folks in Maintenance have a thing going with some folks in Stocking."

Billy and Harley could only shake their heads.

Skeet

After lunch, Billy and Harley found themselves teamed up with Skeet to learn how to do the monthly maintenance test on the facility fire pump. Skeet did everything because he didn't want the rookies in his way. As he worked quickly, Harley and Billy were forced to stand off to the side to watch and learn as much as they could.

"Skeet, why is there no safety training?" Billy asked.

Skeet said without looking their way, "You have to be kidding me. Why would we do that? It would eat away production time, and management won't let that happen. Production is what drives things around here. We're just cogs in the wheel. But we take care of our own."

"What do you mean?" said Harley.

"Let's just say if management wants to see us as just parts in the machine, then we'll just take what belongs to us."

"Do you mean steal?" said Billy.

"You sound shocked, college boy."

Billy said, "I'm just surprised that anyone would want to steal anything from here. We get a nice-enough deal through our employee discount."

"Let me explain. A while before you two started here, we used to get a bonus right before Christmas every year. One way Mr. Henry cut costs was by terminating them."

"That must have killed morale around here," Harley said.

"Oh, it did. Mr. Henry tried to soften it by increasing our wages a little, but it didn't compare to what we used to receive."

"I can imagine," Billy said.

"So, since Mr. Henry thought it was okay to take from us, a few of us believe it's okay to take from him."

"What if someone gets caught?" Billy asked.

Skeet said, "No one will. Who do you think knows this place better than anyone—knows how it runs and all of the fine details?"

"The workers," Harley said.

Skeet said, "That's right. We know every process in detail. We know what's working well and what isn't. We know the strengths and weaknesses of this facility."

"Why don't you think anyone will get caught?" Billy asked.

"We have a system," Skeet said.

Who is 'we'?" Harley asked.

Skeet said, "There are a few of us from different departments. The main group of us work in Inventory Control, Stocking, and Maintenance."

"Are they all friends of yours?" Harley asked.

Skeet said, "It's not that we're friends. We just have a shared mission, and that involves getting things we deserve. If the old man wants to cut our bonus, we know how to get it back."

"If you're not friends, how did the group get established?" Billy asked.

Skeet said, "You're a college kid. Think about it. Why would we need someone from Stocking on the team?"

"I'm not sure, because I haven't been around here long," Billy said.

Skeet said, "It doesn't matter if you've been here long or not. This isn't rocket science, kid. What do workers in Stocking do?"

"They take merchandise from the dock, and they put it away in bulk storage back in the tall racks," Billy said.

Skeet said, "That's right. What is so special about that type of work that might help us?"

Harley said, "Two things. Shane told me one thing that bothers him is that he's alone most of his shift except when he gets on the dock to pick up a new pallet of merchandise. Most of his time is spent back in the tall racks, away from people."

Skeet said, "This is a smart man. You should hang around him more, college boy. You might be able to learn a thing or two. That's one thing. What's the other?"

Harley said, "Stocking sees everything that comes through the facility. They know what comes in, and they know where it's stored."

"This man's a genius!" Skeet said.

"What about Maintenance?" Billy said.

Skeet said, "You tell me. Harley got the ball rolling. Think about why Maintenance is a part of the puzzle. Where have we worked since you two have been here?"

Billy said, "Everywhere. We've been in every corner of this facility and outside."

"That's right. And who keeps an eye on us?"

Harley said, "No one that I remember. I just assumed the cameras were watching us."

"What cameras are you talking about?" Skeet said.

Harley said, "They are all over the place. You must know where they are. They are all of those tinted domes you see hanging from the ceiling everywhere."

"They're dummies," Skeet said.

"What?" Billy said.

"Mr. Henry is after one thing. And that is?" Skeet said.

"Cutting costs," Harley said.

Skeet said, "That's right. And he sure isn't going to spend the money he's making on cameras. Cameras are expensive and would take too much from his bottom line. So he hangs dummies in here, trying to make us think we're being watched."

"But how do you know for sure there aren't cameras in the domes?" Billy asked.

Skeet said, "For a college kid, you're not too bright. Maintenance has to be here on weekends once in a while to do preventive maintenance on equipment when the facility isn't running. One weekend, a couple of us on the team checked out the domes. There are no wires running from them. And we also peeked inside a few. They're empty."

Billy could only shake his head.

Skeet said, "So, Maintenance can take merchandise that is either pointed out to us or handed off to us by Stocking. We can leave the building through any door without being monitored."

Harley was amazed at the simplicity and effectiveness of the plan.

Skeet continued, "Now comes the tough question. Why do we need someone from Inventory Control?"

Harley and Billy stared at each other with blank looks.

Skeet said, "That one's a little tougher, so I'll let you off the hook. Inventory Control measures shrink in the warehouse."

"What's shrink?" Harley asked.

"It's how much merchandise turns up missing from inventory counts," Skeet said.

Billy said, "Missing...do you mean stolen?"

Skeet said, "No, it doesn't mean it was stolen. It may appear short because Shipping didn't check an order correctly and said we received everything when we didn't. Or someone in Stocking might have put merchandise away in the wrong location. Or someone in Order Selecting might have picked a wrong item to be shipped somewhere it wasn't supposed to go. There are a lot of reasons why things may not show up right during an inventory count."

"I never thought of that," Billy said.

Skeet said, "Our Inventory Control contact has access to shrink reports. They know what levels Mr. Henry has tagged as potential concerns. As long as shrink stays below a certain number, Mr. Henry doesn't care. He sees it as acceptable loss."

"I wouldn't think any loss would be acceptable," Harley said.

Skeet said, "In a facility this size, things are going to go wrong, so Mr. Henry accounts for that. He doesn't want to spend a dollar chasing a dime."

"So, your team uses the shrink number as an indicator of how much you can steal," Billy said.

Skeet said, "We don't like the word *steal*, college boy. We see it as taking back what's ours. You know, Robin Hood and all of that."

"Okay, then you use the shrink number as an indicator of what you can take," Billy said.

Skeet said, "That's right. And we can take as much or as little as we want, depending on the numbers."

"What do you mean?" Harley asked.

"We know how to fix the shrink number. As I said before, employees are the ones doing the work and who know how to fix problems. We can take a look at a shrink problem and fix it. That drops the actual shrink number and gives us a larger range to take from."

Billy said, "That's amazing. So, you can manipulate loss the company is naturally experiencing to benefit your plan."

"That's right," Skeet said.

Billy said, "How did it get to this point? I know cutting bonuses wasn't good, but wouldn't it work better if everyone worked together to make the company profitable? And safer?"

"We're okay. We look out for one another. Mr. Henry made it clear he didn't want our help. He thinks he has all of the answers. He's made his bed, and now he gets to lie in it."

It Happened

Maintenance had been under pressure to get a Receiving conveyor back up and running. Skeet and three other technicians were called to work furiously to repair damage to the conveyor, which had been hit by a forklift operator. Downtime cost money, so they needed to stop the bleeding as quickly as possible. Billy and Harley were along for the ride.

"How did this happen?" Skeet growled as he arrived at the scene along with his little entourage. He stepped out of his motorized maintenance cart and made a direct line for the damaged conveyor, which ran three feet above the ground with easy access for the work that needed to be done.

A skittish John Stephens approached. "I'm really sorry, Skeet. I was running my forklift over here to pick up a pallet that needed to go straight onto a trailer in Shipping. I was in too much of a hurry, made my turn a little too wide, and hit the conveyor."

Skeet said, "What little bit of time you were trying to save obviously wasn't worth it, because now this is going to cost us some downtime."

John said, "I know. That was a bad call. I'll take it easy next time."

Skeet immediately took control of the work area. He made an initial assessment of the damage and began assigning tasks to the maintenance technicians. "Harley, I might need you in a minute since you know your way around machinery. In the meantime, I need you and Billy to stand back out of the way to watch what we're doing. Just observe. Nothing else."

Billy was fine with that. He was afraid he might be called on to directly assist. At this point, he thought that simply watching was a great idea. He could at least begin learning what the maintenance team did and how they went about their work. Observing would also help him learn a little bit about how the conveyor belts worked.

The next hour brought a flurry of activity as the maintenance team worked in perfect harmony to get the job done. Skeet dispatched technicians for various parts and tools, which were swiftly delivered back to the work area. The maintenance team worked as one cohesive unit rather than as individuals. They danced together, each one anticipating what needed to be done next, stepping in at the right moment for their individual contributions as the work unfolded.

Billy was in awe of what these workers could do. He leaned over to Harley and whispered, "This is a little intimidating. I'm not sure I'll ever get to their level of skill."

Harley looked at him with a slight grin. "No worries. You'll be able to do it. All of these folks were in your boat at some point in their careers. It just takes time and effort. You'll get there."

Harley's words gave Billy some consolation. He still had his doubts as the work continued while he and Harley watched artistry in motion.

The maintenance team had nearly completed their work when Billy noticed a piece of debris caught between the conveyor belt and a drive pulley. It was a shred of packaging left behind from unboxing one of the repair parts. In an effort to provide at least a little support, Billy quietly walked to the conveyor and reached for the packaging material. He tugged on it, but it was tightly wedged.

Harley remained focused on the maintenance team, unaware of Billy's efforts. As the team finished up, Billy pushed the conveyor belt up and reached in to get a stronger grip on the material. At that moment, Skeet, who was not aware of what Billy was doing, turned on the conveyor to test it.

The conveyor belt started quickly, pulling the debris and Billy's arm into the pulley, which immediately brought him to his knees. Shock took over, and Billy became completely disoriented and appeared unaware of what had just happened. The initial rush of adrenaline was soon followed by unworldly pain as he recognized the injury he had just suffered. A primal scream emanated from deep within him. He tried to quickly dislodge his arm but could not remove it. His torso was stretched across the top of the conveyor, and he could not see the pool of blood that bloomed around his knees. An artery had been cut against the edge of the conveyor railing, and life was beginning to leave him.

Billy's scream would live in the hearts and minds of those who had heard it for years to come. It shocked employees to know that such an unearthly sound could come from a human being.

Harley quickly turned and ran to Billy's side. He hugged Billy tightly with his left arm, trying desperately with his right hand to apply pressure to stanch the flowing blood. He whispered into Billy's ear, "I've got you, buddy."

Skeet turned off the conveyor within seconds, but it was already too late. The maintenance technicians ran to do what they could. Reggie called 911 for help, though he was certain none could be given. Billy would be gone well before the paramedics arrived.

"This is Piatt County Emergency Services. What is your emergency?" said the dispatcher calmly.

Reggie said with his head down and eyes closed, "Uhh…we have an employee who just got his arm caught in a conveyor belt. He is…uhh…I think he's dead. We need someone as soon as possible."

"What is your address?" asked the dispatcher.

"We're at 1139 Industry Road in Sanford," Reggie mumbled.

"Someone is on the way."

Reggie clicked off.

Workers who had heard Billy's scream immediately came to the area but did not know what to do. They stood in shock, looking at Billy's lifeless body and watching the maintenance technicians as they responded in vain. The crowd of workers grew silently as the moments passed, many with mouths covered by a hand and eyes open wide, attempting to understand what they were seeing. Whispers and shaking heads began to ripple through the crowd.

"Call Guy!" yelled Skeet.

No one moved. Other than the maintenance technicians attempting to work around Billy, who now realized he was gone, everyone stood frozen in place with their eyes fixed on the tragic scene as its images permanently burned into their minds.

Skeet reached for the radio on his belt and depressed the voice button. "Guy, this is Skeet. We need you at the Receiving conveyor now."

"I'm at my desk in the middle of something," came Guy's voice in response over Skeet's radio.

"Man, we need you here now. We have a major problem. Billy's in bad shape." Skeet's hands were shaking, and his voice beginning to quiver as he paced back and forth with his head down.

"On my way," replied Guy. He knew something was critically wrong when he heard Skeet's final response. He bolted from his desk and ran into the warehouse. Time was a myth as he navigated his way to the receiving dock, his worst fear soon to be realized.

Workers who saw Guy running and were unaware of what was happening stopped what they were doing and began to collect in small groups, wondering what had gone wrong. They had never seen Guy running through the warehouse at full steam.

Skeet turned to his fellow maintenance technicians. "Reggie, we need to cover him up. People can't see Billy like this." Reggie was sitting on a pallet of cell phones with his head in his hands, rocking slightly. "Reggie! We need to cover him up!"

Reggie slowly raised his eyes as the scene came back into focus. "Okay, I'll run to the Maintenance Shop and get a tarp."

Skeet said, "Great, hurry. We have to get him covered."

Reggie made his way to his nearby yellow maintenance cart and sped away.

Guy passed Reggie as he arrived at the scene. "What happened, Skeet?" Guy asked, eyes wide open, face flushed, and breathing heavily from his run.

Skeet stepped to the side and pointed to Billy's lifeless body. Shaking his head, Skeet said, "He's dead, Guy. It happened so fast."

Guy instinctively ran to Billy's side, not registering Skeet's words. Guy knelt down in a misguided attempt to help Billy. Reality began to trickle into his mind as he saw the pool of blood. He was not looking at an injured worker who could be revived. He was looking at a lifeless body.

Guy slowly stood and walked away from the crowd of stunned workers as thoughts began to swirl in his mind. *How could this happen in a distribution center? Fatalities are the things of construction sites and coal mines, not warehouses! How could I let this happen?*

Skeet walked to Guy and said, "Reggie called 911 and is getting a tarp to cover Billy."

Guy turned and saw the group of workers staring at the scene. He walked up to the two remaining maintenance technicians. "Go get the welding curtains from the Maintenance Shop. We can't let everyone see this." The technicians boarded their carts and raced to the Maintenance Shop as Reggie returned.

Reggie pulled the yellow tarp from his cart and walked tentatively toward Billy's lifeless body. Skeet joined him to unfurl the tarp, and they gently draped it over the conveyor belt, letting it hang down to the concrete floor. They backed away, each thinking—hoping—that this was a dream from which they would soon awaken.

Guy approached the crowd of workers who were still looking at one another in disbelief. Choking back a breakdown and with tears beginning to surface at the edges of his eyes, Guy said, "I know this is a lot to take in, but I need you to move away. For now, take a break. Head on up to the lunchroom. I'll be up shortly."

As the workers began to comply slowly, the maintenance technicians arrived with the welding screens. The screens were placed in an arc around the conveyor belt to prevent people from viewing the scene where Billy's body lay.

To avoid communications being heard by others who had radios in the facility, Guy retrieved his cell phone and called the receptionist, informing her that an ambulance would soon be arriving and that she needed to direct it to the receiving dock. "What happened?" she asked.

"Just do it," Guy said and clicked off.

When the ambulance arrived, the receptionist directed it as requested. The paramedics quickly entered the building through a nearby door where drivers had their delivery paperwork checked. Guy met them and went along as they quickly pushed their stretcher, leading them to the scene. They removed the tarp and checked Billy for all vital signs, soon confirming that he was dead.

The paramedic with "Kinsey" on her name badge asked Guy for assistance. "We need to disassemble the conveyor belt so we can remove the body."

"We'll help," said the paramedic whose badge read "O'Neal."

Guy turned to Skeet and said, "Help them."

"Let's go, Reggie," Skeet said as he walked toward his maintenance cart where his toolbox rested.

Skeet and Reggie worked gently along with the paramedics to remove whatever conveyor parts were necessary so that Billy's arm could be pulled free. The paramedics spread a black nylon body bag on the concrete floor and laid Billy's body on it. Kinsey zipped the bag closed. With Kinsey at Billy's head and O'Neal at Billy's feet, they lifted him onto the stretcher and strapped him in securely.

"We are really sorry for your loss," O'Neal said as they pushed the loaded stretcher toward the ambulance.

Guy could only stand and stare through an open dock door at the ambulance as it drove away. Worse was the realization that he must now call Billy's family with the news of what had happened.

Gathering the Troops

The headlines in the Champaign newspaper read, "Axeon Unsafe—Employee Killed." The article went into great detail on Guy Henry's history with the company, their increased profitability, and their lack of focus on safety. Local Axeon customers read the paper, while distant customers read the story on the Internet. Guy immediately began to realize the business repercussions of what had happened. Axeon customers might soon search for another company to supply them. Customers might distance themselves, not wanting to be associated with a business partner that seemed negligent enough to experience a fatality.

Guy called a 7:00 a.m. leadership-team meeting the morning following the incident. The team was composed of the maintenance manager, Frank Perry; the human-resources manager, Liz Tyler; the operations manager, Ted Jenkins; and the director of finance and accounting, Lea Newberry. The leadership team had been designed to provide cross-discipline input on all significant issues facing Axeon. The team was now in uncharted territory.

Louis Fairchild was a new and temporary addition to the leadership-team meeting. Louis was a labor attorney whom Liz had used on previous employment issues that required legal assistance. Never had she imagined that she would be calling him for assistance in managing a fatality.

Once everyone was settled into the Axeon conference room, Guy called the meeting to order. Tension was thick, and emotions were on the surface. "I guess we'll start with Frank giving us a summary of exactly what happened," he said.

Taking a deep breath with fingers interlocked on the tabletop and looking nervously around the room, Frank began, "John Stephens was operating a forklift yesterday afternoon when he lost control and struck the Receiving conveyor belt. The conveyor went out of commission and we had a lot of product coming in, so we had to get it back up and running quickly. I sent Skeet and Reggie out with a couple of other maintenance technicians to repair the conveyor. Billy Ellis was assigned to shadow Skeet to learn maintenance, so he tagged along. Skeet was finishing up the repairs when he turned the conveyor on to make sure everything was working properly. He didn't realize Billy had reached in to pull out a piece of packaging material. When the conveyor started, Billy was pulled into the drive pulley, and it appears he was cut against the edge of the conveyor belt frame."

"What was the packaging material from?" Guy said.

Frank said, "It was left behind by one of the maintenance technicians who had unboxed, unwrapped, and then handed a replacement part to Skeet. The technician must have put the packaging material on the conveyor instead of throwing it away."

"I guess Skeet did not look around to make sure everyone was clear of the conveyor before starting it up," Guy said.

Looking down at his hand, Frank said, "That is correct. He knew where the other technicians were but did not expect Billy to be involved."

"On the forklift incident that started all of this, Liz, what training records do we have on Mr. Stephens?" Guy said.

Clearing her throat, Liz said, "He was hired ten months ago as an order selector—he picked and fulfilled orders. He had an opportunity to move into Stocking, which required him to operate a forklift. He engaged in on-the-job training with Sylvia McDonald, who is one of our seasoned forklift operators and has been with us for ten years. Eventually, she thought he was okay to operate the forklift on a solo basis, and he has been doing that for five months."

"What actual training documentation do you have?" asked Louis.

Liz said, "We don't really keep documentation on training. We know which employees we can trust, and we connect new hires with them for on-the-job training."

Louis said, "That's a problem. From a legal perspective, if it isn't documented, it didn't happen. Do you have a written forklift training program or anything that maps out what employees must do in the training process to become certified to operate a forklift?"

Liz replied, "Not really. We trust our seasoned employees and have an informal process to bring new hires up to speed."

Louis said, "That's another problem. A process needs to be in place to uniformly train and certify forklift operators. That way, you are assured that each one has been properly trained and certified before being released to perform independent work."

"Was there anything wrong with the forklift?" Guy asked.

Frank replied, "No. We have preventive maintenance records on it."

Ted added, "We also have operator inspections on file for the forklift."

"What does your operator inspection file look like?" Louis asked.

Ted said, "We have a couple of months' worth—about sixteen. Operators do them at least a couple of times a week."

"A couple of times per week…how often is the forklift used?" asked Louis.

"Every day," said Ted.

Louis said, "That's yet another problem. Forklift inspections are supposed to occur on each shift by the operator using the forklift, so you should have approximately sixty on file."

Guy asked, "What about the conveyor belt repair? How exactly was that managed?"

Frank said, "Skeet and his technicians went to the conveyor belt and began the repairs. Reggie turned off the conveyor belt, and Skeet assessed the damage. Skeet, Reggie, and the other two technicians took care of the repairs while Billy observed. When all of the repairs were complete, Skeet turned on the conveyor belt to make sure it was operating properly."

Louis asked, "How is the conveyor powered? Did they lock out the conveyor?"

Frank said, "The conveyor is powered by electricity and pneumatically—using pressurized air. And what do you mean, 'lock out'?"

Louis said, "I guess that's a no on lockout. Whenever work is being done on equipment, all energy sources have to be shut off and locked out, where a physical lock is placed on the power switch to prevent the start-up of the equipment while technicians work on it. In this case, four maintenance techs were working on it, so a hasp should have been placed on the controls for the electric and pneumatics with four padlocks—one for each maintenance technician."

"What about Billy?" said Ted.

Louis said, "Billy was in a gray area. He was not actually working on the equipment but was present as part of the team. Conservatively, we should have had locks on the equipment for him as well due to him potentially engaging in work as things unfolded. Since there appears to be a lack of understanding at the table regarding lockout, I assume training has not been conducted or documented."

"That is correct," said Liz.

"And that's another problem," said Louis, slouching back in his chair with his elbows on the armrests, his fingertips touching in front of his face.

"Where do we go from here?" asked Guy as he looked at Louis.

Louis said, "The first order of business is to at least comply with the Department of Labor's reporting requirement. We need to immediately contact the Occupational Safety and Health Administration—OSHA—to inform them that a fatality has occurred. That will be the catalyst for OSHA to send one or more compliance officers to conduct a comprehensive inspection of the facility and investigation of the death."

"They will look at the whole facility?" said Guy.

Louis said, "Yes. A fatality results in what is called a wall-to-wall inspection. OSHA will examine the totality of your health and safety management system to determine how well you comply with all applicable safety and health regulations."

"Where are we on financials?" asked Guy.

Liz said, "We have the appropriate workers' compensation coverage for all of our employees. All costs and any potential death benefits should be covered."

Louis said, "At least we are in good shape there. The problem is that those costs are only the tip of the iceberg. There will also be business loss related to employee recovery time from the mental impacts of the incident, and you may lose customers once the news story spreads. Who will be making the call to OSHA?"

Guy said, "I'll take care of that. Anything else?"

Everyone sat in silence, not knowing what else to say.

"I guess we'll call this meeting adjourned," said Guy. Once everyone filed out of the room, Guy sat by himself, staring at nothing, his mind still numb. The reality of the death and the personal responsibility he held began to settle in.

Coping

Sam and Ruth were devastated. The touch of his hand, the warmth of his smile, the sparkle of his eyes—these things once were but never would be again. A gaping hole was left by a life so quickly and violently taken that only those who experience it can understand. The understanding of what caused their child's death brought no resolution or closure for them. They could only remember the conversation they had had in the backyard with Billy and Kat, thinking that they should have done more to encourage him to take a job somewhere else.

Kat felt the loss of a partner and the life they could have had together, the children they might have had as husband and wife, and the many others Billy might have touched through his teaching career. These things would never be.

Kat sat motionless on the couch of the Ellis home, Ruth and Sam flanking her. The reality of what had happened was yet to settle in. There was still the thought that this was all a dream and Billy would come bouncing through the front door at any moment.

"How could this happen?" asked Kat, still in shock and unable to cry.

Tears had come readily and often for Ruth. Tears streamed down her face as she said, "It's so pointless. It's not like he was off defending our country. He was at a regular job, for goodness' sake."

Sam could only sit in silence, not knowing what to say. He wanted to fix the situation as he had done dozens of times in the past as a husband

and father, but he knew that it was not going to happen this time. He felt helpless.

Kat said, "Axeon is a big-enough company. They should have known how to train Billy."

"They need to pay for this," said Ruth.

"They will, but not what you might think," said Sam.

"What do you mean?" said Kat.

"This is all new to me. I talked with Marsha, our school system's risk manager—she handles safety in our school system. She said that workers' compensation death benefits will be it. A 'sole remedy,' she called it. Said Axeon might pay a hundred thousand dollars or so."

Kat said, "They killed Billy, and it costs them only a hundred thousand? My aunt works at a manufacturing plant, and the EPA fined them three million dollars for leaking some chemicals into a river. I guess it's cheaper to kill a worker than pollute the environment. That's ridiculous."

"I know. She told me getting an attorney would only help to make sure the right death benefits are paid. A hundred thousand…I guess that is what the system says Billy's life was worth."

Ruth said, "I don't care about any money. I just want Billy back."

Kat said, "How else will Axeon be held accountable? Something needs to be done to make sure nothing like this happens again."

"The sad thing is we're not the only ones going through this. Marsha said about five thousand workers are killed on the job *each year*. That's about as many soldiers as we've lost since we went over to the Middle East right after 9/11. I was shocked. It's hard to believe that many people are dying each year at work."

"And nothing is being done to hold employers responsible?" said Kat.

"Marsha said a few things will probably happen. She said the workers' compensation death benefits will have to be paid. She said an OSHA investigation might also result in fines that could range in the tens of thousands to well over a million dollars, depending on what they find. She also said that the Department of Justice could hold certain Axeon folks criminally responsible and prosecute them, but it's up to the government if they want to pursue that path."

"I really don't want to talk about this anymore," said Ruth.

"Yeah, we have a funeral to plan," said Kat, her mind racing with the seeming injustice of it all.

■ ■ ■

Employees were traumatized. The Axeon Human Resources Department had to enlist the support of local employee assistance program counselors to help people work through what they had experienced. Axeon lost 5 percent of its employees the first week. The ones who remained required a great deal of attention to deal with the event. Even though Billy Ellis had been a relatively new employee, they all knew that it could have been them being carried away on a stretcher. It would take months before Axeon would reach any level of normalcy. Harley, Agnes, and Shane consoled one another. They took the loss the hardest.

The three sat in the lunchroom two days following the incident. Harley said, "I never saw anything like this coming. This is just a distribution center. It didn't seem like there was anything that dangerous here."

Agnes said, "Me either. But I guess we were wrong."

Harley said, "Things are dangerous on the farm, but I've grown up around that, so I know what to do to go home safe every night. I think I'm out of here. It happened to Billy. Who knows what might happen next? I still haven't heard anything about safety around this place."

Shane said, "You would think they would be all over it. I'm sure they're working on it."

Agnes said, "Maybe. But too little, too late, if you ask me. I think I'm gone, too. I can't risk anything happening to me. I have to put food on the table. I have kids depending on me."

Shane said, "I have to stay. I have a baby on the way, and it took me long enough to get this job. I can't leave it now. They have to be doing something about safety. You can't have someone get killed and then just sit on your hind end."

Harley said, "Maybe, but I can't risk it. I'll have to make a go at the farm again. I would rather do what I can there and at least be able to go home with all of my body parts working."

Agnes said, "I checked with my friend Mary, and she said there is an opening at the call center she works at. She talked to her boss about me, and things look promising. The pay isn't as good, but it's a lot safer there than what I'm now seeing here. I'm with Harley on this one. I need to go home healthy every night."

Shane stood and went over to refill his empty coffee mug. "I can understand that. I need to hang around and ride the storm out. Things will get better."

"Keep telling yourself that," said Harley.

The Investigation

Billy's death resulted in an immediate visit to the facility by the Occupational Safety and Health Administration. Two compliance officers had been assigned the responsibilities of conducting a comprehensive inspection of Axeon Logistics and an investigation of the fatality. They arrived the morning following Guy's report of the incident to OSHA.

The inspectors arrived in Axeon's front lobby and spoke to the receptionist. "Hello, my name is Megan Denardo, and this is Sid Jessup. We are here to meet with Mr. Guy Henry."

"Do you have identification?" the receptionist asked.

"Yes," said Megan. She and Sid showed the receptionist their Department of Labor ID cards, each in a small, bifold leather holder.

The receptionist carefully examined each ID card. "Please take a seat. I will call Mr. Henry."

As the IDs were being handed back, Megan asked, "Would you like to make a copy of our cards for your records?"

"Uhh…yes, sure," said the receptionist. She quickly stood up and walked to the machine behind her desk, making copies of the cards. She then returned them.

Megan said with a polite smile, "Thank you. We will be right over here." She and Sid took seats in the small waiting area.

The receptionist dialed Guy's number. "Mr. Henry, two people from OSHA are here to see you." After a brief pause, she said, "Thank you," and hung up. "He will be right out," she said with a forced smile.

"Thank you," said Megan.

Moments later, Guy entered the reception area. "Hello, I'm Guy Henry." He extended a welcoming hand.

Megan responded with a firm handshake. "I am Megan Denardo, and this is Sid Jessup."

Guy turned to shake Sid's hand and said, "Please, you can follow me. We will go back to my office." They walked through a door, briefly through the warehouse, and into Guy's office. Megan and Sid made their initial impressions of the Axeon facility as they followed Guy, taking in the environment with each step.

Once in his office, Guy directed the compliance officers to two chairs in front of his desk. He had added one since Billy's interview. "Can I get you anything?" he asked. "Coffee or water?"

Megan said, "No, we're fine. We can go ahead and begin, as this will likely be a long day or two. Sid can start us off by giving you an overview of what we will be doing over the course of our inspection and investigation."

"Thanks, Megan. Mr. Henry…"

"Please, call me Guy."

"Sure. Guy, over the course of our visit, we will accomplish two objectives. One is to investigate the fatality that occurred two days ago involving Mr. Billy Ellis as the victim. Our investigation will include a thorough visit of the incident scene. We will interview all workers who were involved. We will also review all applicable safety program material that directly pertains to managing risks associated with the incident. This includes safety policies, programs, training documentation, and all paperwork generated as a result of implementing safety programs. Our second objective is to conduct a comprehensive inspection of your facility. We will inspect all areas to determine how well you are identifying and responding to hazards and your general efforts in protecting your workers."

"I understand that an investigation needs to be done on the incident, but why do you also need to conduct a full inspection of our facility?" asked Guy.

Sid answered, "Due to the severity of any incident involving a fatality, we need to inspect all aspects of your facility to identify issues that could result in a future similar incident. The goal is to ensure that you become aware of things that need to be addressed to protect all of your workers."

Guy said, "I guess that makes sense. What do we do from here?"

Sid said, "We would like to start with the scene of the incident. Can someone from maintenance meet us at your receiving dock so we can take a look at the conveyor where the incident occurred?"

Guy said, "Sure. I can walk you out there and will have our maintenance manager, Frank Perry, meet us there."

They stood to walk out of the office as Guy radioed Frank to tell him to meet them on the receiving dock. Guy led Megan and Sid into the main production section of the building and directly to the receiving dock, catching curious stares from workers as they went.

Frank was waiting for them as they arrived on the receiving dock. He was afraid to shake hands because they were damp with sweat—not from working, but from pure terror at meeting people from OSHA. "Hi, I'm Frank," he said with a slight wave.

"Nice to meet you, Frank. I'm Megan, and this is Sid. If you don't mind, please walk us through everything that happened leading up to the incident and everything that occurred at the time of the incident."

"You bet," said Frank as he turned to lead them to the conveyor belt, which was now fully repaired and operational. "One of our forklift operators, John Stephens, was coming back to the receiving dock to pick up a pallet of merchandise to take to Shipping. He misjudged the amount of clearance he had and struck the conveyor with the mast of his forklift. If this conveyor belt is down, it has a huge impact on our production, so once I found out about the incident, I sent four of our maintenance technicians out to assess the damage and repair it. Billy was a new hire, and we sent him along for the ride so he could learn what we do and how we do it."

"How did Billy know where to go and what to do?" asked Megan.

"Billy was assigned to shadow our most experienced maintenance technician, Skeet Davis," said Frank.

Sid asked, "What training did Billy receive to begin working in your department?"

Frank said, "We use on-the-job training. Skeet is our best, so we paired Billy with him."

"Okay. Go on with everything that happened," said Sid.

Sid and Megan quickly typed notes into their computer tablets. As Guy watched, his heart rate began to increase. Frank said, "Sure. Skeet was the lead on the work, so he directed everyone."

"Who was 'everyone'?" asked Megan.

"In addition to Skeet, there was Reggie Forrester, Skeet's primary partner; Jim Davis; and Sally McAllister," said Frank.

More note-taking, and Guy began to shift on his feet. Frank wanted this to be over quickly, as his bowels began to quiver.

"Okay, go on," said Megan.

"Skeet worked with the other maintenance technicians to repair the conveyor. Once everything was done, Skeet turned it on to make sure it was running properly. That is when Billy was pulled into the main drive pulley."

"What caused Billy's arm to be pulled into the conveyor?" said Megan.

"One of the technicians left a piece of packaging material on the conveyor that must have gotten caught as they worked the belt back and forth. Billy was trying to pull it free when Skeet started the conveyor."

"Were the maintenance technicians equipped with locks to lock out the conveyor while they were working on it?" asked Sid.

"No. All of our maintenance technicians talk to one another while work is being done, so they normally know when the belt can be started."

"Who was supposed to be communicating with Billy?" said Megan.

"Skeet told Billy to stand back and watch, but I guess Billy thought he would pitch in and try to help by collecting trash."

"Do you have a written procedure that maintenance technicians are supposed to follow when locking out conveyor belts?" said Megan.

"No. Our technicians just know what they are supposed to do."

Megan said, "To sum things up, it appears Billy was assigned to shadow Skeet as a form of on-the-job training. Billy was not provided with any maintenance-specific job training. Maintenance technicians did not have lockout equipment, and there is no written procedure for locking out the conveyor while it is being worked on."

"That's about right," said Frank, desperately trying to find a way to take some of the sting out of the situation.

Sid said, "Well, that shortens up our investigation a little bit, since there are no documents for us to review. Could you show us the investigation form that presents your findings from the incident?"

Frank turned to Guy with a puzzled look on his face.

Guy glanced at Frank, realizing they now had another problem. He said, "We don't have any documentation. We just talked through everything in our leadership-team meeting."

Megan and Sid cast brief looks at each other with just a hint of frown. Though they tried to put on polite faces, too many issues were surfacing—and they had not yet been in the facility for an hour. "To stay on task, let's find a room where we can interview each person involved in the incident," said Megan.

Guy said, "You can use our conference room. It's quiet there. No one will be able to hear your interviews, and you will not be disturbed."

Sid said, "That sounds perfect. Frank, we appreciate your time. You have been a lot of help."

"No problem," said Frank, though he was thinking, *Not sure I would call it help.*

Guy led Megan and Sid back to the front-office area, where he steered them to the conference room. "Please sit wherever you like. Who would you like to speak with first?" he asked.

Megan said, "I believe we need to speak with Skeet Davis, Reggie Forrester, Jim Davis, and Sally McAllister. The order doesn't matter."

Frank said, "Okay, I will ask Frank to send them up and make sure they all speak with you. I'm not sure what he has them working on, so I'll check and get things moving." Frank turned to leave, and Megan and Sid made themselves comfortable.

Skeet was the first maintenance technician to enter the room. "Hi, I'm Skeet," he said, offering a handshake and an awkward smile.

Shaking his hand, Megan said, "Hi, Skeet. I'm Megan, and this is Sid."

"Nice to meet you," said Skeet.

Sid said, "Have a seat, Skeet. We have a few questions for you. This might take a while, so I hope we will not disrupt too much of your work."

Skeet said, "No, we're okay. Things are running smoothly today."

Megan said, "Could you tell us your full name? We'll be typing a few things into our tablets as we go along, so don't let that worry you. We just need to make sure we accurately record things."

"No worries. Do what you have to do. My full name is Ralph Samuel Davis. Skeet is my nickname. When I was a kid, my dad always said I was as annoying as a mosquito, or 'skeeter,' as we called them. So, I was called Skeeter when I was young, and it was later shortened to Skeet."

Megan and Sid typed quickly as they nodded their heads. Sid said, "Okay. Then we'll keep calling you Skeet, if that's okay."

"You bet. That would be best."

Megan asked, "Skeet, could you tell us about the training you received to do your job when you were first hired to work for Axeon?"

"I didn't really receive any. I already knew what needed to be done. I've been around the block, so there wasn't anything I didn't already know. I had been in maintenance for years before being hired here, so I was already up to speed."

"Did you receive any type of new-hire orientation?" asked Sid.

"Yeah, but we mostly went over benefits, like medical insurance and vacation. That kind of thing."

"Was anything discussed regarding the job you were to do?" said Sid.

"Just the hours I was supposed to work—when I was supposed to clock in and out. Maybe a little bit about all of the things I would be responsible to do, but they knew I was already up to speed on all of that, since they knew my experience."

"Who conducted your orientation?" asked Megan.

"That would have been Liz—Liz Tyler, our HR manager. She's sharp. Knows her stuff."

Megan said, "What about Frank Perry? Was he involved in your orientation?"

"No, not really. Frank knew me from way back. All of the maintenance folks in this area know one another, so Frank already knew what I could do. Not to brag, but Frank knew I could get the job done."

"When did you start with Axeon?" asked Sid.

"That would've been about six years ago."

"What safety training have you received since then?" Megan asked.

"We've talked about the basics to make sure we're safe—like wearing a face shield when we're welding. We know how to work safely and make things happen."

Megan asked, "What about on the day of the incident? What do you know about lockout?"

"We don't have to lock things out, because everybody knows to stay away from moving parts while work is being done."

"How was Billy supposed to have known to stay away from the conveyor?" asked Sid.

Skeet dropped his head. "I guess he thought he could chip in. But I told him to stand back and watch. He hadn't been around long enough to see how things are done."

"Do you think training might have helped him to become aware of that before he was assigned to shadow you?" said Sid.

"I guess so."

The interview continued as they walked through each detail of the incident. Skeet's account of it matched the one Frank had already provided. Sid and Megan continued to type information into their tablets. A cold sweat began to break out on Skeet as the interview progressed, but it concluded with a polite, "Thank you for your time," and Skeet stood and quietly walked away.

In the next three hours, the remaining maintenance technicians were interviewed, all with similar results. They indicated that they had not been formally trained to perform their jobs and that no safety training had been provided. All accounts of the incident matched, giving Megan and Sid confidence that they had an accurate chain of events leading up to the incident and what had caused it to occur.

The Inspection

Axeon Logistics was situated on 124 acres of land, of which the building occupied eight hundred thousand square feet. The north entrance included a reception area, management offices, a small conference room, and a large break room. All of these rooms flanked a hallway that led from the reception area to the main warehouse, with a layout that was a large square divided into quadrants. Guy had arranged for Frank to escort Megan and Sid through the facility for the inspection.

Frank met them on the warehouse floor at the door that led out of the office area. He asked, "Are we ready to go?"

Megan said, "I believe so. We have the investigation wrapped up, and now we need to walk through the entire facility."

"No problem. I'm yours for as long as you need. I'll start by giving you an overview. As you can see, we are standing in the middle of the front of the warehouse. As we look out into the warehouse, you'll see twelve dock doors stretching out along the front wall to the left and twelve stretching out to our right, divided by the open area we're standing in. The doors to the left are for Receiving, with which you are already familiar. The doors to the right are for Shipping. When product comes in through Receiving, one of two things can happen. Most of it is taken by double motorized pallet jacks back to bulk storage, where it is stocked. The other thing that can happen is that single boxes might be pulled and placed on a conveyor to go back to Quality Control, where products are inspected, weighed, and measured. After Quality Control is done with the product, it is placed back on a conveyor belt and sent to Stocking, which is in the back left part of the building."

"I can understand inspecting items, but why do you weigh and measure them?" asked Sid.

"That helps us to make sure we have the proper cubic feet and weight when we go to send out a shipment. We need to know about how much space we have to send out orders in a given trailer, and DOT has limits on weight, so we need to make sure we do not overload a trailer and then have the driver get hit with a fine at a weigh station out on the highway."

"Interesting," said Megan.

"Stockers take merchandise from bulk storage and break pallets apart to keep pick slots filled in the back right corner of the building, where order selectors fulfill orders. They pull individual items from pick slots and either put small items into a tote until it is filled and put the tote on a conveyor, or they might pull a larger box, such as one that holds a gaming system, and put it straight onto the conveyor. The conveyor will then transport all of the order down to the shipping dock, where everything is assembled and secured on pallets, which are then loaded into a trailer for delivery. If a customer has a large order of a certain product, we will pull that straight as a palletized load from Stocking and bring it directly to the shipping dock on a forklift."

"Sounds like a fairly straightforward operation," said Megan.

"It is. If you think about it, everything makes a big circle. Product comes in at the receiving dock, goes back to Stocking, is then taken over to Picking, and then comes back up front to Shipping."

"Where is your maintenance area?" said Sid.

"It's all the way in the back center of the building."

Sid said, "Good. We'll need to spend some time there."

Wonderful, thought Frank.

Megan said, "Okay, let's start our inspection. Maybe we can go ahead and start with the receiving dock, since it sounds like that is the beginning of the process."

Frank led them to the receiving dock area, where production was well underway. Eight of the twelve dock doors had trailers backed into them with motorized pallet jacks being driven quickly into and out of the trailers. Workers were busy on the floor, scanning bar codes into the computerized warehouse management system and unloading boxes onto the conveyor belt.

Sid and Megan walked slowly through the receiving dock, periodically stopping to tap notes into their tablets. Frank became a little more anxious each time he saw the tapping. Megan stopped and turned to Frank and said, "I don't see any forklifts around here right now, and you didn't mention them as being part of the receiving operation, but we found during our investigation that it was a forklift that damaged the Receiving conveyor. Why was a forklift in the area?"

"That generally doesn't happen. Forklifts usually stay in the shipping dock or are used in the maintenance area. But once in a while, we have to use them somewhere else. The day of the incident, we were running tight on getting an order shipped out. Product was being delivered that had to go right back out on another trailer. When that happens, we have to send someone from Shipping over here to the receiving dock to pick up a pallet and get it over to the trailer being loaded."

Sid said, "That would be considered a nonroutine task. That's something that happens once in a while, apart from day-to-day operations. Tasks like that can increase the chance of an accident occurring since workers don't typically perform them. It's a good idea to revisit safe work procedures for non-routine tasks once in a while in preshift department meetings to keep workers aware of what needs to be done."

Megan said, "You can also have more formal discussions regarding non-routine tasks prior to points in the year when your production cycle might change and could increase the possibility of nonroutine tasks."

Frank said, "Yeah, like before the Christmas rush, when we have a spike in production hours and work a lot of overtime."

"Exactly," said Megan.

"Okay, I believe we can move on to the next area," said Sid.

"We'll head straight toward the back of the building, where you'll see our bulk-storage area."

They walked to a part of the building that looked like a large library where there was row upon row of four-level racking. Each section of racking was approximately eight feet wide and accommodated two pallets stored side by side for a total of eight pallets per section. Each row extended two hundred feet toward the back of the building, with twenty-five sections of racking on each side.

Frank said, "The operation here is very straightforward. Stockers pick up pallets from the receiving dock using the double pallet jacks. They drop the pallets near the front of an aisle. Another group of stockers then picks up individual pallets and places them in the appropriate slot using a reach lift. We'll see reach-lift operators as we walk through the area."

As they walked through the fourth aisle, they saw a reach-lift operator traveling toward them. They stopped and watched the operator as she brought the lift to a stop and raised a pallet of merchandise to the third level of racking. A reach-lift is similar to a forklift, but instead of the operator sitting, she stood in an enclosed compartment. The design of the reach lift allowed this operator to store a pallet of merchandise by making tight turns in the confined area of the aisle. She leaned out to ensure clearance and expertly maneuvered the pallet into place. She retracted the forks, lowered them to the ground, and sped away for her next pallet.

"She is good at what she does," said Sid.

Frank said, "Yeah. We only allow our most seasoned operators on reach lifts. It can be tricky to navigate back here."

There was more tapping on tablets as they continued to walk. Frank's heart rate quickened.

After walking each aisle of bulk storage, Megan said, "I believe we have seen everything we need to see. We can move on to the next area."

"Okay, we'll take a detour into the maintenance area, since it is nearby. Then we can pick up in Order Selecting."

Frank led them into the maintenance shop, where Sally McAllister was working on a reach lift. The maintenance shop was a two-thousand-square-foot block in the back center of the warehouse. The area included shelves for storing parts, a variety of tools and equipment, segregated work areas for different types of repairs, and a small office.

Frank said, "The office is mine. If we can, we bring things from the floor back here to repair and then take them back out. We have assigned areas for certain work to be done. Over there in the back corner, you see Sally working in the lift-maintenance area. We park lifts there for repair or preventive maintenance. Hot work is done in the other back corner. We try to keep welding in that area and guarded against sparks getting to combustible material and people seeing the flash. The front areas here are used for general work, like fabricating machine guards or other things we might need around the warehouse."

Sid and Megan slowly walked through the maintenance shop, tapping on their tablets as they went. They looked at each tool, closely examined each work area, and stopped to observe Sally as she worked on the reach lift. "Okay, I believe we can move on to Order Selecting," said Megan.

Frank led Megan and Sid across the back of the building, where they arrived at the end of the order-selecting area. "This is the first of two pick modules," said Frank.

Megan and Sid looked down a structure that was two stories high and was as long as the stocking racking. A conveyor belt ran down the center of each level, with order selectors on each side of the belt rapidly pulling product from slots, placing it in totes, and pushing full totes onto the belt. Teams of stockers were busy on the back side of the gravity-flow pick slots, replenishing product.

Megan and Sid climbed a set of stairs to the upper floor and slowly made their way down the pick-module line, careful not to disturb workers as they passed. They stopped occasionally to pick up items on each of the four levels of pick slots. Once they reached the end with Frank in tow, they descended a set of stairs and made their way through the first level, again randomly picking up items and setting them back in their slots as they went.

When they reached the end of the floor-level line, Frank said, "I noticed you picking up product once in a while. Were you just checking to see the type of things we process?"

Sid said, "No, we were checking to see how heavy different items were. A critical issue in an area like this is ergonomics, which is how the body of a worker interacts with the work environment. When lifting items, it is better to have heavier items between a worker's knees and shoulders. That way, less stress is placed on a worker's body, which could lessen exposure to strains and sprains."

"Interesting," said Frank.

Megan said, "Since you weigh all items coming into your facility, you could use that information to assign heavier items to pick slots that are on the second and third levels. That would prevent workers from having to reach low to first level or high to the fourth level to retrieve heavy objects."

"Sure, we can check into that," said Frank.

Megan and Sid continued their inspection by walking along the back wall and repeating their work in the second pick module. When they were done inspecting the second pick-module, Megan said, "Okay, I believe we are now ready to finish up in Shipping."

Frank led them along the side wall of the warehouse to the shipping area, where the pick-module conveyor belts converged in a number of shipping lines. He explained, "All product that has been pulled in the pick modules is directed to Shipping by conveyor belts. Workers in Shipping stack totes and boxes onto pallets. A forklift operator picks up a completed pallet and carefully drives it to the shrink-wrapper."

Megan and Sid watched as a forklift operator delivered a full pallet of merchandise to a machine, where the pallet was gently lowered onto a platform. A shrink-wrap operator turned on the machine, causing the pallet to rotate while wrap was dispensed and wrapped the product as the shrink-wrap arm followed a vertical path up and then down again. The secured pallet was then removed from the machine by the forklift operator, who then staged the pallet near a trailer that had been positioned in one of the shipping-dock doors.

Megan said, "This appears to be a straightforward operation as well. Unload off the conveyor, stack it onto a pallet, shrink-wrap it, stage it for loading, and then single pallet-jack operators load it onto a trailer."

"Yeah, that's about it," said Frank.

"From an ergonomic perspective, the conveyor belt offload is at a good height for workers to pull totes and stack them, but they have to bend down until they fill the first layer or two of the stack," said Sid.

Megan added, "An option here is to get a hydraulic palletizer, where the pallet begins at a good height and then lowers as totes are stacked onto it, keeping a good working height for loading the pallets."

"Sure, we could look into that," said Frank.

As in the previous departments, Megan and Sid slowly walked through the shipping dock, observing every part of the operation—with more tapping on their tablets as they went. Frank shifted nervously where he stood.

Megan returned to Frank and said, "I believe we've seen everything we need to see. Sid and I will go back into the conference room and go through what we have observed, and then we would like to have a closing conference. We would like to at least meet with Guy, but we welcome as many members of the leadership team as would like to attend."

Frank said, "Sure, we can make that happen. I'll go and get with Guy. Let us know when you're ready, and we can meet in the conference room."

The closing conference began. Guy had wanted to present an environment of support and inclusion, so each member of the leadership team had been asked to attend.

Megan began, "I would like to thank Frank for guiding us through the facility today. He was very helpful in showing us every part of the building and answered all of our questions."

Frank responded with a nervous smile.

Megan continued, "We will be unable to present to you our final report, but we would like to walk through some of the key opportunities for improvement. As has already been discussed regarding our fatality investigation, two areas for improvement include lockout and tagout and powered industrial truck training. Workers, such as those in maintenance and anyone who might need to clear conveyor belt jams, need to be provided with locks and trained on the proper shutdown and control of energy that powers equipment being worked on.

"Powered industrial truck training and certification can include workers who operate forklifts, motorized pallet jacks, stock pickers, and reach lifts. Here's something that can help you. An issue that came up during our inspection today is the question of addressing nonroutine tasks. We came to understand that when Mr. Stephens entered the receiving dock on the day of the accident, he was engaged in an activity that does not normally occur through daily shipping processes."

Guy said, "That is correct. Workers in Shipping do have to go to Receiving from time to time to pick up a full pallet, but it doesn't happen that often."

Megan said, "Focusing on ways to keep safe operating procedures on the minds of workers can help to reduce the potential for accidents. As we discussed with Frank during the inspection, you can do this by revisiting nonroutine tasks periodically during preshift meetings."

"We can do that," said Ted, the operations manager.

Megan continued, "We noticed a number of other opportunities during the walk-through. Some of your exits are blocked with what appeared to be random storage."

Ted said, "Yeah, we run out of space sometimes and place things in atypical areas. That's an easy thing for us to get under control."

Megan said, "I used an app on my tablet when we were walking throughout the warehouse and noticed in some areas that sound levels are above what they should be for workers not to be wearing hearing protection. I did not see any workers wearing earplugs or earmuffs in those areas. Am I correct in assuming that workers remain in the jobs we witnessed for a full eight-hour shift?"

"Yes, that is correct," said Ted.

Megan said, "An opportunity there is to implement a hearing conservation program among affected workers. You can also consider job rotation as a way to reduce worker exposure in loud work areas as well as install noise-dampening systems that can lessen the amount of noise to which workers are exposed."

Sid said, "Similar to what Megan just mentioned related to job rotation, we noticed some issues related to ergonomics. An ergonomics program would be in order due to the amount of manual product handling that occurs. The way in which workers interact with the work environment can play a big part in the occurrence of strains and sprains as well as a host of cumulative trauma issues, such as carpal tunnel syndrome. Repetitive motion can create significant and long-lasting issues for workers. We mentioned some ideas to Frank as we conducted our inspections, but in addition to those, one option is to rotate workers into different tasks so they do not use the same muscle groups throughout the course of a day."

Guy said, "That could impact our production. Workers tend to become really good at what they do when they stay on a given job all of the time."

Sid said, "True, but job rotation might actually increase production. Consider a worker who is in Picking all day. His or her production might be high during the first hours but then taper off later as the worker becomes bored or tired. Rotating that worker into another department to do something different might keep them more alert and engaged. Morale might also increase when workers see that they have value to the company beyond a single task."

"I guess that might be true," said Guy.

Ted said, "Yeah, I never thought of it that way. Could be worth a try."

Megan said, "Back to storage. We noticed two other issues there. In addition to a blocked emergency exits, when we accessed your electrical panels, we had to wedge our way between different things that were piled near the panels and motor control centers. A three-foot clearance needs to be maintained in front of these areas so they can be quickly and easily accessed. We also noticed that a number of sprinkler heads are obstructed by storage that is piled too high. That will limit water discharge from sprinkler heads in the event of a fire."

"We can definitely work on those issues," said Ted.

Sid said, "One other item we want to review with you is injury and illness record keeping. We understand that you have had some previous minor injuries, such as cuts that required stitches, in addition to the fatality. You are required to maintain documentation of each injury and illness that meets OSHA's definition of a recordable case. The primary categories are other recordable, restricted work, lost time, and fatalities.

"In general, other recordable cases are accidents where an employee has to go off-site to a doctor for treatment. Restricted work cases are those where a doctor determines that an injured worker cannot perform his or her regular job for at least one day following the accident—for example, because of not being able to use an arm or having to avoid standing for long periods of time. A lost-time injury is one in which the doctor determines that the worker must stay home to recover for at least one day following the day of the accident. A work-related fatality is self-explanatory. All of these incidents must be documented first on the OSHA 301 form or a company document that requires the same information. Either serves as an accident investigation form. Some information from those must be transferred to the OSHA 300 form, which is a log of injuries and illnesses for a calendar year. Information from the OSHA 300 log is then included in the OSHA 300A form, which is an annual summary that can be submitted to the Bureau of Labor Statistics to be used for national data collection."

Liz said, "We plan to post a safety manager position. I can work with the person we hire to manage recordkeeping and bringing injured workers back to work."

Sid said, "We will not go over everything right now, but in general, you need to build a safety management system that complies with all applicable regulations and includes plans for managing everything. We have been discussing some of the highlights, but the notice of violations you will later receive from us will detail all of the exact legal issues you need to address."

Megan added, "One final question from us. Do you have a safety incentive program?"

"We do not, but the idea has come up in some initial discussions following our accident," said Guy.

Megan said, "You will find that there is a wide spectrum of safety incentive programs to choose from. One thing to keep in mind is that if you do set up a program, ensure that it does not deter workers from reporting injuries."

Guy said, "What do you mean? I thought the point of a safety incentive program was to avoid injuries."

Megan said, "That is true, but you need to deeply explore the activities you want to encourage in a safety incentive program. For example, some of them are set up to reward employees if the facility or a department works a certain amount of days without an injury. That can put pressure on workers not to report workplace injuries to avoid coworkers losing the reward. Instead, you could provide rewards for things that workers proactively do to improve safety. For example, you could set a target number of legitimate recommendations for improving safety performance. Other activities could be worker participation in a safety committee or perhaps involvement in safety inspections or incident investigations."

Guy said, "That makes sense. I understand what you're saying."

"I believe we are done with everything, unless anyone has any final questions," said Megan.

Guy asked, "When can we expect to receive your final report?"

Megan said, "We have ninety days to send the notice of violations to you. We send it by registered mail to ensure we have a record of receipt. From that point, you will have thirty days to respond. Usually, our area director has an informal conference with you before everything is brought to a close. You can use that opportunity to request any changes to the notice of violations and arrive at a settlement."

"We thank both of you for working with us through all of this. I believe we can improve what we are doing," said Guy.

Megan said, "I agree. If there is nothing else, we will be on our way."

Megan and Sid collected their things and left the conference room. An overwhelmed leadership team was left behind.

The Settlement

The notice of violation arrived much quicker than expected through registered mail. Though OSHA had ninety days to deliver the document, it only took twenty. It was clear that there was a sense of urgency: OSHA wanted workplace safety addressed at Axeon as soon as possible.

The receptionist walked the manila envelope to Guy's office, where she found him engrossed in his computer screen. She said, "You might want to take a look at this. It says it's from the Department of Labor." She gently laid it on his desk and quietly made her exit.

Guy's pulse rate began to increase. Not only had the notice of violations arrived sooner than expected, but it also appeared to be rather thick. Not a good sign. Guy retrieved his letter opener from a Duke stadium cup he kept as a souvenir from attending the 2015 bowl game win over Indiana. He wasn't feeling much luck from the cup rubbing off on him as he slowly inserted the blade and made his way across the top of the envelope. He let out a slight groan as he freed the notice from the envelope, taking in its girth. Depression engulfed him as he quickly flipped through the document, taking in the volume of citations and the financial penalties attached to each one. He reached for the office phone on his desk and punched four numbers quickly to contact the receptionist. "Please call Louis. We need to set up a meeting for this afternoon."

Louis arrived late in the afternoon with a grim expression. He was not looking forward to reading the documents that awaited him on Guy's desk. "Not good," said Guy as he offered a handshake.

Louis shook firmly with his right hand while accepting the notice of violation in the other. He sat in a chair in front of Guy's desk and began to leaf through the pile of pages: thirty-five in total. "We have our work cut out for us," he said.

"I assume all of this is under attorney-client privilege," said Guy as he took a seat behind his desk.

"To an extent. Our discussions are covered under privilege, but the content of these documents could be produced by the government if someone files an open-records request that is granted."

Guy dropped his head. More bad news. He couldn't imagine what it would be like if any of the information in the notice of violations was made public. He might lose even more customers. The question of the viability of Axeon Logistics began to cross his mind.

Louis began to walk through the basic issues. "OSHA can cite four classifications of violation. *De minimis* violations are those where a violation has technically occurred, but there is no significant exposure to injury. We have none of those. 'Other than serious' is a violation of the law where moderate exposure to injury exists. We have five of them. 'Serious' violations are those where a significant exposure to injury exists, and we have seven. The highest level is that of 'willful' violations. These are violations where you knew of a hazard and did nothing to protect workers. We have six of those, bringing us to a total of eighteen violations."

"That's a lot to deal with," said Guy.

"It could be a lot worse. The picture being painted through these citations is that you have no safety program, which, from what I gathered during our previous meeting, is true."

Guy dropped his head again and nodded. "Aside from the obvious issue, we haven't had any really bad injuries with the exception of a couple of broken bones from an isolated fall, so I thought everything was going okay."

"It appears you were wrong. OSHA now knows exactly what is going on here. Or maybe I should say, what is not going on. There are no written programs. There are no written procedures. There has been no safety training."

Again, Guy simply nodded.

"You are also looking at a total of approximately two million in fines," said Louis.

"We'll go out of business. We don't have two million lying around."

Louis said, "Don't go there yet. There are some things we can do."

"Like what?"

"Negotiation. This notice is a starting point. Everything in the notice appears to be in order. Each citation is appropriately referenced. For example, 29 CFR 1910.147 is properly referenced in the 'willful' violation related to not locking out the conveyor during the incident. You were also cited under the General Duty Clause for not addressing ergonomic issues where employees are exposed to poorly designed work environments where strains and sprains or other similar injuries could occur from poor posture or repetitive motion."

"What is the General Duty Clause?" asked Guy.

"When the Occupational Safety and Health Act was first passed, it included a clause with very broad language that basically stated that employers are responsible to provide a safe environment for workers. OSHA can use that clause as a basis for a citation when it sees something that is unsafe, but there is no specific OSHA law that addresses the issue. There is no law that specifically addresses ergonomics, so OSHA uses the General Duty Clause to support a citation. Think about it…with the large volume of dynamic workplaces in the United States, it would be impossible to develop a law for every individual safety issue. Current OSHA laws hit most of everything, but the General Duty Clause is a catchall for any identified hazard where a specific law does not exist."

"Seems unfair. How am I supposed to know about everything? I'm not a lawyer."

"Ignorance of OSHA laws is not a defense, so we can stick a fork in that right now. There are plenty of avenues for you to become aware.

You could go to trade-association training sessions and conferences on workplace safety. You can access safety webinars online from the computer right there on your desk. You can take safety college classes online. You have a maintenance manager and a human resources manager. You could also hire a safety manager. OSHA itself has a website with a ton of information for you."

Guy said, "I get it. You don't have to keep going. Obviously, I've dropped the ball here."

"You could say that."

"Where do we go from here?" Guy asked.

"Like I said, the notice of violations is a starting point. We now have thirty days to create a response. I would recommend we ask for an informal conference to be set up with the OSHA area director to see if we can reach a middle ground. We need to look at how we can reasonably argue for a reduction in the level of some of these violations and proposed penalties in exchange for a commitment to safety on the part of Axeon."

"What would that look like?"

"First, you could offer, as part of a settlement agreement, to hire a full-time safety manager as a member of your leadership team. Your lack of knowledge of workplace safety issues is significant, and hiring a safety manager would be the quickest way to get you to where you need to be. That person could work to create a great deal of material referenced in a number of citations in conjunction with your workers and members of management. The safety manager could advise you on an ongoing basis on what needs to be done regarding workplace safety."

Guy asked, "Where does the money to pay for a safety manager come from?"

"Your budget. Right now, you are looking at two million in penalties. We could ask for a reduction there in exchange for hiring a safety manager. OSHA could see it as a good-faith effort to get on the right path and might see your money being better spent there instead of on penalties. Your return on investment would be immediate through lower penalties as well as in future years, with someone to lead the way and ensure that Axeon's environment doesn't engender a situation similar to what you currently face."

"So, that person would run safety for me," said Guy.

"Yes, but that does not mean you can abdicate responsibility for safety. You, the rest of management, and your workers must work together. It will not all be on the shoulders of the safety manager. That person will help keep you pointed in the right direction and coordinate all safety efforts across your departments, but everyone must be involved."

"I get it. What else?"

"We don't have much of a position to argue for lessening the severity or level of the penalty on merit, since you do not actually have much of an organized safety management system. However, as with hiring a safety manager, we could propose that reduced penalties would allow more money directed toward workplace safety improvements. That could include allowing payroll hours to cover safety training for your workers and purchasing the necessary equipment for implementing various safety programs, such as personal protective equipment and installing fall protection."

"Either way, we're paying," said Guy.

"That's right, but you should try to direct the money toward improving safety rather than flushing it by paying a penalty. I believe you realize what you need to do now, and the corrective measure of enforcing a penalty will not have the impact that improving safety could have on the floor."

Guy said, "I'm definitely learning my lesson. Guess I let this one get away from me. I can't believe I let someone die on my watch. I just never thought that big of an incident could happen. We've had a few accidents, but nothing near this." Guy lowered his head once more and examined his interlocked fingers on his desk.

Louis said, "The priority now is to learn from it and make sure it never happens again. Do what we can to make sure benefits are paid to the family, and put your shoulder into building a strong safety management system."

"You've got that right. What now?"

"I will draft a response to the notice of violation, and we can set up an informal conference with the area director of OSHA. With a more minor set of violations, we could have conferenced over the phone, but I believe we need to do this one face-to-face to demonstrate good faith with our proposal for reduced penalties in favor of channeling resources into improving safety. The economy is tough, and the area director, Jim Shephard, is good to work with. He's been around the block and should understand what you're up against. You're not the first employer lacking a developed safety management system."

"Let's do it. I'll be there whenever the area director can get it on his schedule."

■ ■ ■

The informal conference occurred two weeks later in Jim Shephard's office. Guy shed his typical khakis and golf shirt in favor of a suit and tie for the occasion. Jim welcomed Guy and Louis into his office with a gracious smile. Though Guy's hands were clammy, Jim's handshake calmed him. This was not Jim's first rodeo. Many employers had been in this place in past years, pleading their cases in hopes of limiting the damage and getting things on track to protect their workers.

Jim had a reputation in the safety community of understanding the situation from both sides of the fence. He understood the needs of the worker and the pressure that organizations were under to stay competitive and turn a profit. He was well versed in operational issues, so embellishment of the facts was limited, as well as the aspirations of company representatives and their attorneys.

The office was furnished with the typical government fare—appointments designed for work, not to impress. Jim led Guy and Louis to a round conference table positioned a short distance from the expansive desk. There would be no power play from Jim. He didn't lord over Guy and Louis by opposing them across the desk from his position of influence. The round table indicated that no seat was greater than another. They were all on the same level, working toward the most productive outcome.

As he sat down, Guy said, "We appreciate your time in meeting with us, Mr. Shephard. I'm Guy Henry, the director of operations at Axeon Logistics."

"Please, call me Jim."

"Sure," said Guy.

"I'm Louis Fairchild, legal counsel for Axeon."

"It is a pleasure to meet both of you," said Jim.

Megan Denardo entered the room. "Sorry I'm running a little late," she said with a crisp smile.

Jim said, "Gentlemen, I have asked Megan to join us, as she was one of the primary compliance officers who conducted the investigation and inspection."

"Hi, Megan, nice to see you again," said Guy—as if "nice" was an appropriate word to use under these circumstances.

Megan said, "Sid can't make it this morning. He's out on another inspection."

Jim said, "No worries. I'm sure your input will be more than enough for us to get where we need to go today. Let's get started with an overview of where we stand. Megan, if you would, give us an overview."

"I will be glad to. The incident that initiated our investigation and inspection was a fatality. Billy Ellis was a college student who was hired to work in the Maintenance Department at Axeon Logistics. On the day of the incident, he had been assigned to shadow a senior maintenance technician. While experienced maintenance technicians were working to repair a damaged conveyor belt, Billy reached to free a piece of packaging debris. The conveyor was started at that moment, and Billy was pulled into it, severing an artery, which resulted in his death.

"Without going into detail on each of the citations in the notice of violations, Sid and I basically found that Billy had not received safety training for the work he would be doing. He also did not receive task training to work in the Maintenance Department. Instead, Axeon utilized on-the-job training as their primary training method. Further investigation and the following inspection revealed that Axeon had no safety management system to speak of that should have addressed complying with safety regulations and managing safety issues at the facility. In general, there was no evidence of workplace safety effort."

"Do you gentlemen have anything to add?" asked Jim.

"That about sums it up," said Guy with a slight quiver in his voice.

Jim said, "Gentlemen, as you now must clearly know, it is the responsibility of each employer to provide its workers with a safe work environment, and it is clear that has not been accomplished at Axeon. The challenge is where to go from here. Right now, we are looking at numerous individual citations totaling over two million dollars."

As he slid a document across the table to Jim, Louis said, "I have been working with Guy and the Axeon leadership team to address the issues identified in the notice of violations. I have drafted a proposal that we believe will allow us to satisfy the spirit of the penalties and provide an opportunity to procure the resources necessary to implement a robust safety management system."

Working hard to maintain eye contact with Jim and Megan, Guy said, "Though the investigation and inspection Megan conducted along with Sid was done under tragic circumstances, we appreciate the work they did, and I now realize what we should have been doing all along. The loss of Billy Ellis has struck all of us deeply, and I plan never to allow anything like this to happen again."

Jim said, "That's a good place to start. Most employers I have interacted with have had some form of company document indicating that their workers are their most valuable asset, but incidents such as this betray such a proclamation."

Guy said, "I understand. And we are no different. We value all of our workers. We have experienced minor injuries in the past that we have managed, but we never considered that an incident like this was possible."

Jim said, "It is difficult to have to learn that lesson this way. The occurrence of only periodic minor injuries does not equal an absence of great risk to workers."

Guy said, "I understand that now. I just wish I could rewind the clock."

"At least we might be able to correct the course from here," said Jim.

"Indeed," said Guy.

"What do you propose?" asked Jim.

Louis said, "In the document, we request a thirty percent reduction in the overall penalty amount. That will allow Axeon to pay a substantial penalty while allowing the redirection of the remaining portion to improving safety."

Jim said, "That is a large requested reduction. What plan do you have to utilize the money?"

Guy slid a second document across the table to Jim. "This document includes our strategy for improving workplace safety. In the near term, we will hire a safety manager. This individual will join our leadership team and will assist us in integrating workplace safety into all our operations. Our human resources manager, Liz Tyler, has conducted a salary survey, and we believe we can attract an experienced professional who can hit the ground running for eighty thousand per year plus fringe benefits. The remaining amount is budgeted across the areas in which we were cited to purchase equipment and provide for other resources necessary to address the issues that have been identified."

"It looks like you've done your homework," said Jim as he leafed through the document.

Guy said, "Yes, sir, we have. I now realize what I did not know before and want to start moving in the right direction."

"What do you think, Megan?" asked Jim.

"Though ignorance of responsibility for safety is not an excuse, I found during our visit to Axeon that there was a simple lack of understanding and a number of misled assumptions regarding worker safety. I believe the level of citations should stand, since there's plenty of safety information available to employers—and because of the obvious hazards

Axeon willfully disregarded. However, the interviews we conducted on-site and the discussion here indicate a sincere desire to address workplace safety."

Jim said, "I agree. Gentlemen, with our attorneys, I will conduct a more thorough review of the documents you have provided. I'll get back with you soon on our final decision. Do you have any questions or anything else to add?"

Louis said, "No, sir. I believe that covers everything."

As they stood, Guy said, "Thank you for meeting with us. We are committed to improving safety at Axeon. We appreciate the opportunity to work with you in making that happen."

Jim said, "We will do what we can. We will be in touch soon. Megan will walk you out."

■ ■ ■

Guy was notified within one week of OSHA's ruling on their proposal. He and Louis met in Guy's office to review the details. As he read through the settlement agreement, Louis said, "Instead of thirty percent, OSHA is willing to reduce the penalty by twenty-five percent."

"What do you think of that?" said Guy.

"Again, it could have been much worse. It's not what we asked for, but it's not a bad deal either. I would advise you to take it."

"I agree. I believe it's time to draw this chapter to a close and move on to getting everything into place to improve safety."

Continuing to read the settlement, Louis looked puzzled. He said, "There is one interesting addition…"

"What would that be?"

"They are requesting that you become an industry spokesperson to endorse the development of safety management systems, to include a discussion of what happened here, complying with OSHA requirements, and integrating safety into a business."

A cold sweat began to cover Guy. The thought of standing in front of other supply chain leadership and airing his dirty laundry had no appeal to him. "I'm not sure about that."

"It's part of the deal, Guy. All you have to do is present at conferences on what happened here and how other industry leaders can work to prevent something like it from happening in their organizations."

"I guess it would be a good thing. I could help other folks in operations become aware of the need to integrate safety into their businesses. In addition to what we will be doing to improve things here at Axeon, maybe a greater good can come from all of this. The loss of life, the depression we continue to deal with…it can be prevented. Let's do it."

Rebounding

Axeon employees had been discussing the incident, and rumors were starting to take form. Liz, the HR manager, had felt it would be best to hold a meeting to stem the emotional tide generating among both workers and managers. Liz encouraged Guy to be transparent about everything, and he agreed. He would be breaking new ground with this meeting, and it would not be the last of its kind. They planned for at least an hour to present what the company was doing and to hear everyone's questions and concerns.

All workers and managers from every department and shift as well as all members of the leadership team would be there. The meeting would be on the production floor in a large open area near the front office; Guy had rented a small portable stage where the leadership team would sit as well as a set of chairs for everyone else.

As workers began to assemble that morning, the low rumble of discussion could already be heard. The leadership team attempted to make a good impression by making as much eye contact with workers and department managers as possible, smiling and waving as everyone entered the makeshift meeting area.

Once everyone was seated and accounted for, Guy stood and started what he hoped would be a constructive dialogue. "Good morning, everyone. I appreciate you being here this morning, as we will be discussing some very sensitive issues. Obviously, we have experienced an incredibly traumatic event. Many of you have taken advantage of the employee assistance counselors to deal with what you have experienced. I want to build on it by addressing with everyone what happened and what we are doing about it. I cannot put into words how tragic the death of Billy Ellis was and the impact it has had on all of us and his family. I can tell you that this event has begun a new chapter in the life of Axeon Logistics."

"Yeah, right," came a voice from the back.

Guy had expected such comments and took this in stride. "I realize that many of you may now have reservations regarding your safety at work. You can rest assured that safety will receive greater attention within our operations. In the past, we have had a few minor injuries—cuts and other things that were easily treated and managed. In addition, we had one fall that resulted in broken bones. I was lulled into a false sense of security, thinking that these less serious injuries meant that we didn't have a lot of safety issues to worry about. We all now know that this was a significantly false assumption."

"You have that right," came another voice from among the workers.

"A guy named Senge came up with the concept of a learning organization a few years ago. The idea is that organizations can and should learn from their experiences. Lessons learned can be applied to help an organization evolve and become a better version of itself. That is going to be Axeon. A tragic series of events led to the death of Billy Ellis. I have worked with our leadership team and OSHA to gain an understanding of what happened and what caused the accident. We have identified a number of critical issues related to your safety. We will learn from them and work to make improvements to protect you. In our company policy documents and in our new-hire paperwork, we indicate that you are our most valuable asset. We have demonstrated that in the wages we pay and the benefits we provide, but we now understand that we have opportunity to improve in the area of workplace safety."

Though workers initially had their eyes cast downward, many were now looking up and listening intently to Guy. He took this as a sign that he was beginning to connect with them.

"I have been doing homework on what we need to do. One thing I have noticed is that a lot of organizations use the slogan 'safety first.' In other words, safety should be the first priority. This sounds good, right? But let's face the facts. What is our number-one priority?"

"Production," came a quick response from among the workers. A murmur of assent immediately followed.

"That's exactly right. We are here to produce. We are here to get product out the door to our customers so that we can turn a profit. That profit is then invested in your wages and benefits, among other things, and will now also be invested in your safety. The problem I faced is how I could I say 'safety first' when in reality, I would be lying to you. After thinking about this for quite a while and doing more homework, I realized that safety should not be a priority, or *first*. It should be a *fundamental part* of how we carry out production. It must become a core value in our operation rather than a simple priority, because priorities might change from time to time. What are some key measures we use to assess production?"

"Quality," came a voice.

"That's right. We measure quality. We work to ensure that our shipments are sent out as ordered by the customer. We make sure that if a customer orders a hundred tablets, fifty smartphones, and forty-five laptops, we ship a hundred tablets, fifty smartphones, and forty-five laptops. How else do we measure production?"

"Volume," came another voice.

"Right, again. We measure the volume of production to make sure we are putting through as many pieces as possible in the time you are working. Measuring volume helps us to ensure we are working as quickly as possible, controlling the cost of what it takes to get product out the door. Going forward, we will also be measuring safety. Safety will not only be a priority, such as in 'safety first.' We will also work to make it a core value of how we carry out our work, similar to the way that quality and volume are integral. It will become a fundamental part of how we do work."

A hand was raised near the front of the group of workers. "How will we do that? We haven't received safety training on our jobs."

"It will be a long road, but we have already begun to chart our course. We will be doing two primary things. First, we will be hiring an experienced safety manager to help us comply with all safety laws that apply to our operation. This person, a member of our leadership team, will report directly to me. This will allow safety to have visibility in all critical operational decisions we make, and I will have direct interaction with her or him on an ongoing basis. Second, we will all work together to integrate safety into our operations through the creation of a safety management system—similar to systems we have in place to manage things like quality, accounting, and human resources. Our system will mean that safety is included in meetings. We will measure our safety performance and train each of you on safety issues that impact you while you work and how you can participate in improving safety. We will identify risks for injury and correct any such problems. I know this sounds like a lot, but if we work together, I am confident we can make safety a part of how we do what we do."

Barbara Sullivan, a seasoned stocker, said, "How will we have time for all of this? We barely have time to do what we need to do now."

Guy said, "We will make the time. We might need to adjust some of our production thresholds in the near term. Similar to what we are doing right now, we will allow time for you to come off the floor to attend meetings and training. For example, one thing we plan to do is to create a safety committee with worker representation from each department as well as a couple of department supervisors. All members will be provided with time to attend safety committee meetings. This will be a shift from our current way of operating. In the spirit of integrating safety into our operations, attending meetings and training will be seen as a part of your job, not an exception. Safety will become part of our jobs, not something separate that we have to work into our day. Just like quality control checks, we will factor in time needed to address safety. That will probably look different for each of you. For workers, it will include time factored into your day for things like conducting pre-use inspections on forklifts and activities where you are actively involved in safety. For managers, it will include things such as conducting safety inspections and coaching on safe work behavior."

Ted Jenkins, the operations manager, added, "We went through the same thing when we implemented quality control. We realized the need to address quality in addition to sheer production volume. We made that happen, and we'll do the same thing with safety. The end result will be a safer work environment for all of us, and we will also be able to provide better service to our customers."

"But production will take a hit," said Barbara.

Ted said, "Actually, production should improve. Say, for example, that someone suffers a minor cut to his or her right hand, requiring stitches. That person can come back to work but cannot work at a normal speed yet. Efforts we place toward safety could prevent injuries in the first place and prevent skilled workers from losing time by being away from their jobs to heal from an injury. A safe worker can continue to work at normal speed. Integrating safety into what we do is a win-win. All of us are safer, and it also has a positive impact on production. It will benefit us, our families, and our business."

Liz, the HR manager, said, "Production can definitely be impacted in a positive way, but a strong message we want to send is that you really are our most valuable asset, and improving your level of safety at work is the right thing to do. In addition to helping our business by remaining healthy and working at your greatest potential, all of you also have things you want to go home and do at the end of the day, whether it is to play softball or work in the yard, or something as simple as picking up one of your children. We want to do our part to make sure you can do those things by providing a safe work environment. Our plan will protect you at work while also helping to improve your overall quality of life."

Guy said, "Let's close the meeting with an opportunity for questions. Anyone?"

Charlie Fortner, a receiving-dock worker, said, "Isn't safety just common sense? I don't see why we have to make a big deal about it."

Frank, the maintenance manager, said, "I guess I used to think the same thing, Charlie. That was up until recently. We had been doing a fairly good job, and I didn't think we had a problem. But now, after Billy…I'm seeing a different picture. Success is achieved by design, not by exercising common sense."

Cheryl Bishop, an order selector, said, "And if common sense was truly *common*, everyone would have it. And we know that isn't true."

A small wave of laughter spread throughout the group.

Frank continued, "You can say that again. And I guess that is what I am getting at by saying success is accomplished by design. Think about production. You don't show up each day and just start doing what you think needs to be done. When each of you was hired, we teamed you with an experienced worker who knew our system so you could learn how to do your job. A lot of that needs to change. We need to design training sessions to fully explain how work is supposed to be done—and done safely. I have learned a lot lately about safety. There is a lot of opportunity for us to improve. Unfortunately, that lesson came at a high price…the life of one of our own. That isn't going to happen again."

Sally McAllister said, "We've made recommendations before that went nowhere. How can we expect things to be different?"

Guy said, "I own that one. I came up in industry believing that management had all the answers. I now realize I was wrong, and that is going to change. Each of you is out there, getting things done every day. You know our processes inside and out, and you are the ones best positioned to provide feedback on how we can be better at what we do. I know it will take a while to gain your confidence, but going forward, everyone in this room will be working together to figure out what needs to be done. The safety committee will be one avenue for routing your recommendations and concerns. In addition to that, you can feel free to speak with your supervisor or any member of the leadership team about safety questions or concerns. A key part of this process is for us to identify hazards and correct them so no one is injured. That will be a team effort. The culture we have will be changing to include safety as a primary component.

I understand that I need to demonstrate this by following through on what I am saying today. You have my commitment. I also understand that we'll need to show some successes in order for you to completely accept things, and I am confident we can do it together."

A slight rumble of conversation rippled through the group.

"Does anyone have any more questions?" After a period of silence, Guy concluded, "Thanks for your time this morning. We'll keep you posted as things develop."

Staffing Up

Liz worked with Guy on drafting a position posting for a safety manager, and they wanted someone with experience to start immediately. They needed someone who could help them develop compliance programs and a robust safety management system. Liz learned of a local chapter of the American Society of Safety Engineers, the ASSE. She shared the job opportunity with the chapter and posted it on the Axeon web page and a number of other employment websites. Liz and Guy were shocked at the volume of responses they received.

"The posting has only been up for a week, and we already have twenty-three applications," Liz said as she and Guy met in her office to review the status of the process.

"Are they all qualified?" said Guy.

"Yes. Our online application system weeds out candidates who answer no to any required question, and we asked for three years of experience. I will go through the resumes to make sure they meet all of our requirements."

"Are they all in the Sanford area?"

"Not all of them. I will make sure they know we do not provide relocation during phone screens, even though we said that up front. At the end of next week, I will sift through the applications for the best candidates."

Guy said, "Sounds good. We want applicants who can show they have improved safety in their previous organizations."

Within the final week, eleven more applications came in. Liz went about the task of narrowing down the thirty-four applicants. Nine were out because of typographical errors on their resumes or elsewhere in their application. Liz was amazed that some did not bother to proofread. Finally, she got down to the nine who had withstood the test of communicating real safety accomplishments. Axeon wanted someone with an established history of driving safety improvement, not someone who simply listed qualifications. Further, they did not want to know only *if* someone had implemented safety programs; they wanted to know how well.

Liz and Ted eliminated six candidates in the phone screens. Two lacked communication skills, and four voluntarily withdrew once they learned that Axeon wouldn't pay for relocation. Three candidates remained.

Two of the candidates who had presented themselves well in the phone interviews were not as confident in person. The first had a difficult time maintaining eye contact with anyone—in formal interviews or in speaking with workers during the facility tour. Liz understood that he did well on the phone interview in a room by himself, but the change in communication skills when they were face-to-face was dramatic.

The second interview was equally disappointing. This candidate appeared confident in the formal interviews—maybe *too* confident. During the facility tour, he sounded somewhat condescending when he talked to workers. It was clear that he thought he had all of the answers to Axeon's safety problems. He was not the team player the company was looking for in a safety manager.

With a potential failed search looming, Guy welcomed candidate number three. "Hello, Mr. Henry, I'm Mandy McKeller," she said with a warm smile and a firm handshake.

"Nice to meet you, Mandy. Please have a seat, and we'll get things started. Liz Tyler, our human resources manager, will be in shortly to join us, but we can go ahead and start."

Mandy took a chair in front of Guy's desk, while Guy pulled his seat around to sit near her, with a third empty chair remaining for Liz. With a slight smile, Guy said, "Tell me a little bit about yourself. Particularly,

I'm interested in how you became involved in safety. I can't imagine that there are a lot of young folks who wake up one morning and say, 'I want to be a safety professional when I grow up.'"

"That's true. Most of us discover the safety profession by chance. I grew up on a family farm about two hours west of Minneapolis. When I was in high school, I joined our little town's volunteer fire department. I loved being there, but I wasn't sure of my chances at making a career of it. I started off in a fire engineering program in college, since that was as close as I could come to the fire arena and have a chance at a good-paying job. Even though I wouldn't be on a fire truck responding to emergencies, I would be designing fire suppression systems for companies to minimize damage. When I was in that program, I heard about occupational safety. I soon found out there was a career where I could prevent injuries and fatalities. I felt like that would be a better fit for me, because I could have a career helping people like I did in the fire department back home."

Guy said, "Interesting. I see that you have been with DataTech for the past four years. Why do you want to change jobs?"

"I was hired into an entry-level safety position with DataTech, and there isn't much room for me to move up. I have had a great experience there and love the people, but I'm ready for the next challenge. I've been working under a safety manager there, and we have done a lot of great work. I believe it is time for me to step out into a role where I can demonstrate more independent leadership."

Liz entered Guy's office and said, "Sorry I'm late. My meeting with some new hires ran a little longer than expected."

Guy said, "No problem. Please grab a seat. Mandy and I were just talking about how she got into safety and why she is talking with us today."

"Nice to meet you in person," said Liz.

"Same here. It's always interesting to actually meet folks you have only spoken with on the phone."

Liz said, "I have a question for you. You indicated on your résumé quite a few data points that indicate an improvement in safety performance at DataTech. What do you believe drove that success?"

"One thing: listening to people. When I first arrived at DataTech, a strong safety-compliance program was already in place, but their injury rates were unusually high."

"I thought complying with OSHA regulations would automatically impact injury rates," said Guy.

"Compliance is one piece of the puzzle, but a number of other things impact the occurrence of injuries. Soon after joining DataTech, I started walking the production floor and learning how different departments functioned. I had a degree in occupational safety, but I needed to fully understand how work was done in order to learn what risks to worker safety existed. The first thing I did was to talk to workers about how they did what they did. They were more than happy to walk me through things on a daily basis. Through those conversations, we began to take a look at what could potentially hurt them as they worked. They actually came up with a lot of the issues and possible solutions. I just had to work on reasonable solutions with management and implement what we could."

"Are you saying that you don't take the credit for the reduction in injuries there?" said Guy.

"Yes and no. I guess I can take credit for going out and talking with the workers to begin the process, but it was actually all of us working together to identify issues and solutions. My safety degree program taught me a lot of the mechanics behind building a safety program, so I was comfortable writing compliance programs and believed my personality was a good fit for the profession. I truly care about people and want to help them go home at the end of the day in a healthy condition so they can enjoy life outside of work. It requires the input of people doing the job, safety professionals, and management to come up with the best solutions to safety issues. I could go out on the floor here at Axeon, look at work being done, and rattle off a list of things to take care of, but I'm not the one actually doing the work. I could come up with some good things to do, but those things would never be great without talking with everyone."

Guy began to reflect on assumptions he had made in his own management style and contemplated how connected he truly was to the work being done on the floor. Maybe he had lost touch with some of the reality behind profit-and-loss statements. If working with employees played such a pivotal role in the success of safety, the same should be true with operations in general. He soon realized that he had just found the new Axeon Logistics safety manager.

Leading the Way

One year later.
Sally Montgomery moved back to Sanford to care for her aging parents. A nursing home was out of the question. She had left Sanford shortly after high school with her science-geek boyfriend, working to support him while he got a degree that had something to do with nanotechnology, but she never really understood a lot of what he shared at the dinner table. He had then landed a job with a lab on the West Coast, thanked her for everything, and left her behind. She had bounced around the manufacturing community, rising to the rank of department supervisor at a plant that molded dashboard parts for the automobile industry. She did not hesitate to move back home when she realized that her parents needed assistance.

After cleaning up breakfast on a Saturday morning, Sally settled in at her laptop to start a job hunt. She responded to an Axeon ad for a Stocking Department supervisor, and things moved quickly. One phone interview and a face-to-face interview and she had the job.

Sally arrived fifteen minutes early for her new-hire orientation. She was met with a warm greeting and friendly smile from the receptionist. "Welcome back, Sally. We're glad to have you on board and are excited you decided to join our team. Come with me, and I'll walk you to the training room where you'll begin new-hire orientation."

Sally followed close behind as the receptionist clicked down the hall. They reached a bright room with rows of tables and a large screen on the front wall with "Welcome to Axeon Logistics" on it in vivid colors.

Liz from HR said, "Hi, Sally, we're glad to have you here this morning."

"I'm glad to be here. I've been looking forward to it."

"Take a seat, and we'll go ahead and get started."

There were ten other new hires in the room, and Sally made her way to an empty seat beside a young man. The nervous look on his face gave her the impression that this might be his first job. "Hi, I'm Sally."

"Hi, I'm Josh."

Sally settled in as Guy started the orientation. "Good morning. I'm Guy Henry, the director of operations here at Axeon Logistics. Welcome to the team. You have a full day of orientation in front of you, so I won't take too long. I would like to introduce a few folks up here at the front of the room who will be walking you through quite a bit of information as the day progresses. First is our human resources manager, Liz Tyler."

"Good morning, everyone. I'll start you off with a walk-through on filling out your benefits forms and explain Axeon's employment policies, such as on vacation and attendance."

"Next is our operations manager, Ted Jenkins," said Guy.

"Greetings. Once Liz is done, I'll walk you through a presentation that will help you understand the flow of our operations and the jobs we do at Axeon."

"Last will be our safety manager, Mandy McKeller," said Guy.

"Hello, everyone. I'll take you through a safety orientation that will provide you with initial information about safety concerns and how we manage safety."

Guy said, "Your orientation today will not be the end of the learning process. You will be given a training schedule that outlines the process of your job-specific training and safety training. Not only do we want you to work productively, but we also want you to work safely. Your job training will equip you with the skills to do your job correctly. It will address things like production expectations and quality. Safety training will make you aware of risks that you face and how you need to respond. In addition to safety training, we also encourage each of you to be involved in safety through things like our safety committee and being involved in inspections. Mandy will cover all of that with you during the orientation. We obviously want to strive for a high level of quality and productivity, but we will do it safely. Our goal is to protect you each day you come to work, because we truly believe and are committed to the fact that you are our most valuable asset."

Seven Principles to Protect Our Most Valuable Asset

Principle One:
Safety Makes Business Sense

FROM THE STORY

Guy learned of the negative financial impact that failing to integrate safety into operations could have on his organization. He was facing well over $1 million in penalties from OSHA, workers' compensation costs, and indirect costs, such as the downtime that workers needed to talk through and process what had happened. In addition, Axeon suffered negative news coverage, resulting in some loss of sales due to customers choosing not to do business with Axeon. However, during the informal conference with OSHA, he learned from Megan how integrating safety into operations can have a substantial return on investment through reducing costs associated with injuries and improving productivity.

■ ■ ■

The marketplace demands an aggressive financial approach due to global competition and rising labor costs. There is pressure to trim operational costs to remain competitive. Expenditures on safety can actually help improve organizational performance and competitive position rather than be simply a cost of doing business. The challenge is to translate the money invested in safety into its impact on the bottom line in an environment influenced by profit-and-loss statements.

The lack of a workplace safety management system and resulting injuries to workers can cause two types of cost for an organization. The first is *direct cost*. Direct costs are easily captured due to their immediately visible nature. Examples are:

- Cost of repairing damaged equipment
- Medical payments for treating an injured worker
- Lost-time workers' compensation wage payments made to an injured worker
- Cost to provide personal protective equipment (PPE) to workers
- Salaries and fringe benefits paid to professional safety staff
- Cost to install safety equipment, such as fall protection systems

The second type of cost, which can be more difficult to capture, is *indirect cost*. This is downstream cost that has to be investigated to be properly quantified. Examples are:

- Loss of sales due to brand damage from an incident being made public
- Loss of production time to investigate an incident or to discuss it with workers
- Loss of quality due to an inexperienced worker replacing an injured worker
- Possible turnover of workers who feel at risk on the job

IMPACT ON SALES AND LOSS OF REVENUE

One way the cost of safety can be viewed is from a simple financial loss perspective. In a given year, an organization might suffer a loss of $200,000 in direct cost due to injuries. Other data may reveal that an additional $100,000 is lost due to accidents resulting in property damage, such as forklift accidents and fires. Indirect cost of loss can add an additional $2 to $4 for every dollar of direct loss (National Safety Council, 2013) resulting in a conservative indirect loss of $600,000:

- $200,000 + $100,00 = $300,000 direct loss
- $300,000 x $2 = $600,000 indirect loss
- $300,000 + $600,000 = $900,000 total loss

This same organization produces a product sold at $50 per unit with a 5 percent profit margin, resulting in $2.50 earned for each unit sold. In order for the organization to cover its losses, the organization must sell 360,000 units. All of the operational and sales effort placed into the business to sell those units, as well as the associated profits, must now simply be diverted to cover loss due to poor safety performance.

DOUBLE-DIPPING

Some organizations may rely on a high percentage of temporary workers. Such a system makes sense from budgetary and operational perspectives. From a budget perspective, a great deal of financial risk can be transferred due to the temporary employment agency assuming the risk for workers' compensation for temporary workers. However, a double-dipping effect can occur if an employee suffers a lost-time injury (the worker is out for at least one day to heal). A given department may require ten workers to maintain full operational capacity. A lost-time injury of five days may mean that a temporary worker covers such an absence. In that case, the organization is in effect paying two workers to perform one job: double-dipping. The temporary worker is paid to perform the actual work while the employee is paid lost-time benefits. For example:

- The cost of the temporary worker to the host employer $15 per hour x 40 hours per week = $600.
- The injured worker earns $20 per hour, and workers' compensation regulations typically calculate lost-time benefits as 2/3 of the average weekly wage. In this case, the calculation would be: $20 x 40 hours per week x 2/3 = $532.80 (additional standard cost of fringe benefits still applies).

One way of analyzing this situation is to consider the employee's wages as money that would have been paid normally, according to the concept that workers' compensation payments are intended to make whole the employee in relation to earnings. Such an analysis would result in a loss to the organization of $600—the money paid to assign the temporary worker to the department to ensure full operational capacity.

WORKERS' COMPENSATION COST

Though direct loss related to double-dipping may occur, other financial cost occurs when managing an injury. Medical bills will need to be paid, which can include:

- Medical services for treating the injury
- Appliances needed by the injured employee, such as crutches
- Physical therapy in the rehabilitation process
- Prescription medications

Another area of expenditure is that of claims management. A workers' compensation insurance company assesses fees to manage the claim. Claim-management cost can include:

- Cost to open a new claim file
- Payment to attorneys representing the employer if the claim advances to the point of legal action
- Use of experts, such as private investigators for surveillance if the claim is believed to be fraudulent

PRODUCTION LOSS

In the previous example of replacing an injured employee with a temporary worker, additional indirect loss could be calculated. Such a calculation could include loss of production if the temporary employee is not working as quickly as the person he or she is replacing. The original employee is typically more productive due to experience in the position, whereas the temporary worker might need to be trained and transitioned into the job. If a temporary worker is not hired, overtime wages might need to be paid to existing employees to do the work typically done by the injured employee.

Indirect loss related to production could also include a calculation of resources needed to transition the temporary worker into the job. The department supervisor might need to spend organizational payroll hours attached to the individual to transition the temporary worker into the job that could have been more productively spent on standard operational and leadership issues within the department.

QUALITY LOSS

Similar to production loss, a temporary or transferred worker might not deliver the same level of quality as that of the original employee. The worker employed by the organization will typically have developed skill sets and work methods over long periods of time. The temporary employee might not be able to work at the level desired. Deficiencies in quality work could result in indirect loss, such as the cost of scrapping material and reproducing parts or products. If poor products are actually delivered to a customer, increased cost due to product returns could occur.

PSYCHOLOGICAL IMPACT ON NON-INJURED WORKERS

Tragic accidents in the workplace can reach well beyond the injured worker. Coworkers can be mentally impacted by what happens. Cost can be generated in production downtime when coworkers stop working to talk with one another or with members of management regarding what occurred. Additional cost might be generated by the need to provide counselors through an employee assistance program or other avenues to ensure that the mental health of all workers is addressed.

BRAND DAMAGE

Damage can occur to your company's image if an accident on your premises is made public. A mass worker injury incident or an explosion can be immediately deemed newsworthy, and the press might arrive. Coverage can quickly reach both individual consumers of your product and business customers. Your brand can quickly become tarnished, resulting in a drop in sales if consumers and business partners move on to competitors.

RETURN ON INVESTMENT

Financial loss related to workplace injuries can be substantial, which indicates a need to invest in workplace safety for economic reasons. Though data can be difficult to gather and is organization specific, some study has been made of financial investment in safety and its return to an organization. Liberty Mutual (n.d.) conducted a workplace safety survey among executives. They found that "61 percent believe their companies receive a return on investment of $3 or more for each $1 they invest in improving workplace safety." Addressing specific examples of cost savings, OSHA stated that as a result of developing a safety and health management system and reducing injuries, "A Fortune Five company increased productivity by 13 percent, while a small, 50-person plant decreased faulty product and saved more than $265,000 with a strong safety and health program" (OSHA, accessed April 24, 2017).

In the examples presented by Liberty Mutual and OSHA, it is clear that investing in workplace safety can have a return on investment. There are numerous ways in which organizations can invest in safety:

- **Payroll.** Allow workers to be away from their jobs during regular hours to receive safety training and engage in safety management system activities, such as assisting in incident investigations or serving on a safety committee.
- **Facilities.** Initiate projects to improve the physical safety of the workplace, such as installing fall protection systems, posting safety signs, and redesigning workstations to address ergonomic risks.
- **Personal protective equipment.** Purchase appropriate and comfortable personal protective equipment (PPE) for workers to wear.

- **Executive compensation.** Include safety performance as an element of executive compensation packages along with other business measures.
- **Staffing.** Employ the right volume of safety professionals to assist in directing workplace safety issues. Undergraduate and graduate university degree programs prepare future safety professionals, and professional certifications such as the Certified Safety Professional (CSP) are also available.

MAKE IT HAPPEN

Research your organization to determine the current levels of direct and indirect loss you are suffering each year due to workplace injuries. As in the areas of human resources, operations, accounting, and maintenance, determine if you have appropriately qualified professionals working to manage safety within your organization. Work with your professional safety staff to determine a strategy to strengthen safety as a component of your organizational culture. If you operate a small business, assign safety as a professional responsibility to a member of management and provide training opportunities for the worker to increase expertise in all aspects of workplace safety management system development and implementation. Begin, continue, or increase your financial investment in safety. Measure your investment over time to quantify your return on investment in safety so that strategic decisions can be made on future safety investments.

Principle Two: Comply

FROM THE STORY

The OSHA inspection revealed that Axeon Logistics had made no effort to comply with OSHA regulations. Axeon addressed safety informally and had simply reacted on a case-by-case basis to any minor injuries. Following the fatality incident, the leadership team decided that it had the options of working through compliance with existing human resources or to hire a safety professional. The company's experience of recovering from the fatality and the gap in its technical safety knowledge led it to hire an experienced safety professional who could immediately begin driving compliance efforts.

■ ■ ■

Building a firm foundation is essential in making safety happen and allowing you to grow to a stage of operational excellence. This step in the process is a necessity if you hope to build workplace safety into your daily processes and organizational culture.

WRITTEN PROGRAMS

Written programs and policies serve as the guiding element as you strive to prevent loss. Good comprehensive written programs take a tremendous investment of time and energy. They explain in great detail what you do in relation to different workplace safety topics. Workplace safety issues to consider might include:

- Emergency action plan (evacuation and accounting for employees)
- Hazard communication (chemical use)
- Lockout/tagout (maintenance on equipment)
- Powered industrial trucks (forklift operation)
- Electrical safety (work on electrical panels and equipment)
- Fire safety (sources of fire and preventive measures)
- Machine guarding (protecting workers from moving parts and pinch points)

You will need to evaluate your business to determine what programs are required by law based on the activities within your operations.

TRAINING

Once you have defined your list of programs and generated the written program material, you will then need to train workers and management on issues that apply to them. Written programs in a nice binder on a shelf or neatly placed on a website is a first step toward compliance. The second step is to ensure that the company communicates what the programs contain and what responsibilities different people hold within your organization.

Where feasible, training should include classroom discussion and practical skills exercises. Theory on adult learning tells us that adults retain more information when they can do an activity during a training session. Yes, PowerPoint has become a tremendous tool for conducting training; it is quick and easy to put together a few slides with bulleted lists of information and maybe add a few photos or pieces of clip art to liven the slides up a little. However, as a rule, you should never think that a PowerPoint presentation has done the job. You may need to use such a presentation to initially communicate a body of information, but you should follow it up with practical skills exercises.

When training a group of workers on your lockout procedures, you may have bulleted lists or photos depicting the process on a slide. Take the group out to a machine after discussing the process in class. Demonstrate the lockout procedure and then allow each of them to experience it. The same can be done for a large spectrum of training topics.

Planning should go into making the training as interesting as possible. Do not allow the topic of the material to dictate the level of excitement in the training session. This is a pitfall to which many trainers fall victim. They walk into the session knowing that something is a tough topic to present, such as hazardous materials training, and they allow that negativity to transfer to the class. Attendees pick up on it, and the session is a disaster. See such topics as a challenge and find ways to motivate and energize attendees about them.

ACCOUNTABILITY

Every person in your organization who has been trained or received communication regarding a safety policy must be held accountable for carrying out the information he or she has received. Allowing unchecked behavior that is not consistent with your organization's requirements will undermine your safety efforts and do great harm. Accountability should apply to everyone, from the newest employee to the highest ranking member of management.

A struggle in accountability is determining what it looks like. A very common and fundamental version of accountability is a basic corrective action process. This includes a series of documented discussions with workers and management who are found to be in violation of company requirements. The level of violation may be based on the severity of the infraction. Individuals are told clearly what they did wrong, what they need to do to get back on the right path, and what will happen if they fail to do so. You must also be willing to terminate an employee if matters evolve to a stage of great severity.

Consistency must be maintained throughout an accountability process. Management and workers should not be treated differently. An infraction is a deviation from company requirements regardless of who committed it.

VALUE ADDED
See workplace safety not just as a legal compliance issue, but as something that adds value to your organization by improving organizational function. Value is also added in relation to your bottom line and to the quality of life of your employees. You will reap financial rewards through lowered cost of loss. There will be fewer lost workdays due to injuries and fewer repair-and-maintenance costs from accidents resulting in property damage. This helps your organization to function better. Productivity can increase if you maintain an environment where workers feel comfortable coming to work each day. Workers will also recognize your efforts to protect them, and you will become an employer of choice when you offer workers a safe work environment that results in a higher quality of life.

MAKE IT HAPPEN
Complying with federal, state, and local safety regulations is a matter of corporate responsibility. Industry leaders must exercise discipline in ensuring that they understand which regulations apply and that programs and policies are in place to ensure compliance. Ethically, it is the right thing to do to provide a safe work environment for all workers. From a regulatory perspective, it is the corporate and legal responsibility of industry leaders to ensure compliance with all applicable regulations.

Industry leader personal responsibility for safety has been elevated to the level of criminal prosecution, as was seen in West Virginia when a mining executive was criminally prosecuted and sentenced to prison for negligence—failing to provide a safe work environment for miners. Though such prosecutions are rare, an agreement signed between the US Department of Labor and the Department of Justice has encouraged holding industry leaders individually accountable for workplace safety (US Department of Justice, 2016; Morrison, 2016; US Department of Justice, 2015; *EHS Today*, 2015; *Safety & Health*, 2015).

Principle Three:
Teach Them

FROM THE STORY

Axeon Logistics provided Billy, Agnes, Harley, and Shane with no formal safety or job training prior to starting work. On-the-job training was used as an informal method to transition new hires into the work environment. Realizing the problem, Guy led a much more robust orientation meeting at the close of the story, telling the new hires that they would receive both safety and job training soon after the newly developed orientation meeting.

■ ■ ■

Both workers and management need to be taught how to work safely. We can never assume that workers and managers have organically learned how to work safely. If we could, we would not see the devastating number of injuries and fatalities that occur each year in the workplace. Safe work performance is accomplished by design through clear communication of performance expectations to workers and managers and equipping them with the knowledge and skills to meet those expectations.

THE TRAINING DILEMMA

Safety training can be easily conducted, but for it to be effective, a great deal of thought needs to be put into it. A dilemma we face is that the individuals within our workforce have differences that we must consider before we decide on a training methodology. These include:

- **Different learning styles.** Some people prefer to see and touch actual objects in the learning process, while others prefer to sit quietly in a room and absorb information through reading or listening.
- **Different generations.** The eras in which people have lived can impact how they prefer to learn. For example, according to Cekada (2012), workers from Generation X prefer a casual training environment, while Baby Boomers prefer a traditional training environment.
- **Different cultures.** Geographic and organizational cultures can influence a training session, such as the degree to which the culture drives trainees to participate in activities or respond to questions.

With these variables in mind, it is interesting to note that a great deal of safety training occurs in a uniform format. Workers might be gathered in a meeting room where they are walked through material in a PowerPoint presentation. They may sign a training log and take a brief quiz on the material. Such activity may satisfy regulatory requirements, but did learning actually occur? Due to the number of variables that can affect the learning styles of a given workplace population and a desire of managers to truly educate workers, how do we get there from here?

ADULT EDUCATION

To answer this question, it is important to first understand two key principles of adult education (Elias and Merriam, 2005; Lindeman, 1961). The first is that adults prefer to have control over their learning rather than have it forced on them. They want to manage what they learn and how they learn it.

The second principle is that what adults learn must apply to their personal life experience. In other words, adults must see a reason for learning something and what it means to them before they authentically engage in the learning process.

Giving adults control over their learning and making personal application in a training experience help to set the stage for designing effective training. However, the challenge of designing training strategies is compounded because of the broadening generational gaps in today's workplaces.

THE MULTIGENERATIONAL WORKFORCE

As we've noted, the generation to which each worker belongs can have particular impacts on training (Cekada, 2012). Understanding the learning needs of each of the primary generations represented in a workplace can help determine which training methodologies might be most effective. Here are some examples of training preferences for each generation:

- Silent Generation (1937–1945) and Baby Boomers (1946–1964)
  - Prefer traditional training where the trainer presents information with little trainee interaction
  - Enjoy sharing their experiences that indicate how the material presented in the training session applies
  - Prefer small classes
- Generation X (1965–1976)
  - Prefer a casual training environment
  - Desire a training environment where they can ask questions to clarify various issues presented in the training session
  - Like to have feedback provided on their performance to ensure they are performing tasks properly
- Generation Y/Millennials (1977–1992)
  - Prefer a visual training environment where they can see things being discussed rather than read about them

- Prefer training information to be presented in snippets, with time provided to allow them to explore further information independently or in a group
- Benefit from small group discussions
- Like immediate feedback on their performance of tasks in which they are trained

NEUROSCIENCE APPLICATIONS

Medina (2008) approached learning from a neuroscience perspective. Training sessions can be greatly improved through a basic understanding of how the human brain functions. Some of his findings, which he refers to as Brain Rules, can be directly translated into designing productive training experiences.

- **We don't pay attention to boring things** (p.71). Though this is not an earthshaking revelation, it does highlight the need to address issues such as death by PowerPoint that may plague many training sessions.
- **Repeat to remember** (p. 95). Training sessions can provide opportunity for workers to commit information to short-term memory by repeating critical information, whether by verbally reciting it or through performing tasks.
- **Remember to repeat** (p. 121). Training should not conclude at the end of a formal training session. Information can be committed to long-term memory through remembering to repeat important information and job tasks in the manner in which they were presented in the formal training session.
- **Stimulate more of the senses** (p. 197). Identify training activities that can engage listening, seeing, and doing rather than simply dispense information through one-way communication.
- **Vision trumps all other senses** (p. 221). Training will extend well beyond the formal training session. Though workers need to see things in training sessions, they also need to see what they have

been trained in be effectively modeled in the workplace. Behavior can deviate into unsafe action if they see something in the workplace being done differently from the safe work procedures they were taught.
- **We are powerful and natural explorers** (p. 261). Training can be used to tap the workers' natural desire to learn rather than considered a necessary evil. Workers are natural explorers, and training can channel their energy into authentic learning experiences for a safer and more productive work environment.

ADULT EDUCATION IN THE CLASSROOM

I trained workers in industry and later transitioned into teaching in the college classroom. In my research (Dunlap, Dudak, and Konty, 2012), which analyzed Bloom's Taxonomy, used in the classroom, and Kolb's experiential-learning model, used in adult education, I sought to create a synthesized model for integrating principles of adult education in the classroom. Our model was successfully tested and includes the following principles:

- **Select**. Rather than strictly prescribe learning activities, allow adults to select alternative aspects of the learning process that facilitate their learning styles.
- **Reflect**. Allow adults to reflect on their selection of tools or methods to ensure that they have made the right decision.
- **Apply**. Allow adults to apply what they have chosen.
- **Verify**. Ask adults to decide if what they chose and used was appropriate for the intended task.

For example, let's see how this process can be used in personal protective equipment (PPE) training. Let's say that workers are provided with a scenario in which they would need to use eye protection and an array of equipment to choose from, such as safety glasses, goggles, and a face shield. They are asked to select which they believe is the most appropriate. They then reflect on their selection by considering the various hazards that could cause an injury to the eye. They could then make application by properly putting on the eye protection they have selected. With the eye protection on, they could verify the effectiveness of their selection by walking through the hazards that have been identified to see if they made the appropriate choice. Such an exercise can actively engage them in and analyze the decision-making process as well as help them to translate that process to daily work activities.

MAKE IT HAPPEN

Reimagine safety training as a process rather than an event. A one-size-fits-all approach is not effective if learning is to be practically translated into the work environment. There are far too many variables among individuals, as previously discussed, that make a single training methodology challenging.

- **Compliance Training**
    - The Occupational Safety and Health Administration dictate safety training frequency and content in a number of their regulations, making training an act of corporate responsibility. However, latitude is given as to how the training can be conducted.
    - The training environment should take differing learning styles into consideration. As I've noted, a standard, trainer-driven presentation in a conference room may be appropriate for employees from the Silent or Baby Boomer generations, while Generation X and Millennials prefer a hands-on environment where they can demonstrate tasks and receive feedback.
    - PowerPoint can be used beyond simply presenting a glorified outline. Though such routine use might be sufficient for workers from the Silent and Baby Boomer generations, slides can present problem-posing scenarios that ask workers to interact to come up with solutions, which may appeal to Generation X and Millennials.

- Computer-based training can also satisfy differing learning styles. For example, OSHA's free eTools provide online training on a limited number of topics; they include some interactive opportunities. You can also use PowerPoint for self-running, point-and-click, computer-based training presentations that employ visual images, audio narration, and interactive exercises.
- **Skill Development**
  - Tailor an Individual Development Plan (IDP) for each worker according to what he or she must learn to do his or her job safely, taking learning style preferences into account. Training methodologies can then be developed and delivered for maximum learning. IDP information can include what needs to be accomplished during initial training as well as how the ongoing training process should proceed in skill development by using task observation and coaching.
  - Select the right training environment. Though some safety skill development activities can occur in a training room, such as how to read the hazards of a chemical on a Safety Data Sheet (SDS), a great deal of skill development will need to take place in an actual work setting for complex tasks, such as learning how to safely operate a forklift. When safety training is seen as a process, the work environment can also be considered a training environment with a continuing need to observe and provide feedback to workers while they perform tasks. Such activity will lessen the gap between what workers are initially trained to do and what actually occurs on the job.
  - Practical skills exercises should be used to allow workers the opportunity to demonstrate proficiency. For example, though the components of a fall protection system might be discussed in a training room, practical skills training using the equipment develops skills in the safe use of safety equipment and execution of safety procedures.

- Provide opportunities for selection in the ongoing training process. Though workers in more recent generations might like to receive feedback on how well they are performing their work safely, other generations might prefer to discuss safety issues related to their experiences. Again, consider differing learning styles when structuring ongoing training process activities.

It will be a challenge to become comfortable with the idea of everyone not receiving the same training. The content must be the same, but the manner in which the content is delivered can be agile in addressing varying learning styles. A one-size-fits-all approach to training delivery can satisfy basic legal requirements for safety training but can also be counterproductive, with less than optimal learning and application of material on the job. Though establishing a diverse training system to accommodate different learning styles is challenging, workers will be much more willing to receive the necessary information and thus learn the material better and perform their jobs safely.

Principle Four: Engage Them

FROM THE STORY

Billy had been engaged in safety while working in his previous position at the mall under the supervision of Ms. Ferguson. At Axeon Logistics, he encountered a culture that did not welcome such worker participation in safety. The disconnect between management and workers was further manifested in the elaborate scheme for the theft of product as explained by Skeet. All of this supported a culture of division and distrust. Later reflection on the value of engaging workers in safety caused a shift in the organizational culture of Axeon to include workers and managers in making safety recommendations and in the decision-making process.

■ ■ ■

A fundamental aspect of organizational success is employee engagement. This principle also holds true in the specific area of workplace safety. Benefits to engaging workers in workplace safety efforts include:

- **Ownership.** Worker engagement instills ownership. If workers are part of the development and implementation of safety processes, they are more likely to execute them than if they are simply forced

to comply with organizational programs and policies in a top-down environment.
- **Feedback.** By simply talking with workers who perform various tasks, management can gain valuable insight into unique safety issues that workers face each day. Together, management and workers can arrive at the best solutions to problems that are encountered.
- **Effectiveness.** Worker engagement is a safety success factor. The more workers have an opportunity to engage in safety program issues, the more likely they will be to follow through on working safely, which will result in fewer injuries.

Decades of research have indicated the need to engage workers in our processes. The benefits in doing so include increased quality, productivity, and employee satisfaction. Engaging employees can be expanded to the realm of workplace safety in an effort to prevent accidents and loss of assets. There are many ways to engage employees in loss control activity.

SAFETY COMMITTEES

Safety committees can be established that are composed primarily of hourly workers. These committee meetings provide a forum in which issues can be discussed and input to upper management determined. There are a number of variables to consider when establishing a safety committee:

- ***Bigger is not better.*** You can use the typical ratio of nine hourly employees to one member of management for committee membership composition with representation from ever primary operational group and shift. Excessively large committees may become bogged down in endless discussion due to the wide spectrum of perspectives and opinions held. Limiting the size of the group improves the timeliness of decision-making.
- ***Stay on mission.*** Committees should have a clearly defined mission to keep them focused on appropriate activity. The mission

of a safety committee is, in general, to improve the degree of health and safety performance within an organization. The committee should focus on issues that cause injuries or property damage. The mission should be supported by specific goals for each year that focus on the most pressing safety issues. For example, if workplace observations and incident investigations indicate a theme of strains and sprains, then appropriate goals should be established to target that theme.

- **Beware of the donut eater.** Committee members should have clearly defined roles and responsibilities, and they should be held accountable for their assigned activities. The committee should generate a clear action plan for members who do not demonstrate active participation. These "donut eaters" are those who gladly show up for meetings to partake in the refreshments but offer no substantive value to the group. Seek to include those whom you believe will provide valuable input and move less participative members off of the committee. The members of the committee also present a branding issue. For workers to accept the safety committee as legitimate, it must be composed of workers and managers held in high regard throughout the facility.
- **Take action.** Management must respond to the safety committee's recommendations. If a recommendation cannot be acted on, management should provide a thorough response regarding why action cannot be taken, or if it will not be taken until a later date. Such open communication and dialogue can assist in building trust between workers and management. Improvements to the work environment that result from safety committee recommendations will help to encourage the committee as it sees the impact of its work.

RESPONSE TEAMS

Volunteer emergency response teams can provide employees with an opportunity to participate as well as provide you with a tremendous resource for managing a crisis. First aid, cardiopulmonary resuscitation

(CPR), and automated external defibrillator (AED) training provided by the American Red Cross or the American Heart Association can serve as a strong foundation for equipping response team members.

If such a team is established, you should determine if compliance with OSHA's blood-borne pathogens regulation is required. This regulation requires certain training and precautions to be taken by employees who have occupational exposure to blood or body fluids. This may become an issue if it is expected for emergency response team members to treat employees who have been injured and have produced blood or body fluid. The OSHA regulation provides for protective measures to be taken to prevent the spread of blood-borne pathogens, such as HIV or hepatitis.

Community emergency response team (CERT) training is an additional avenue to consider if establishing an emergency response team. The Department of Homeland Security has established this training opportunity and may fund it through your local fire department. Lessons learned from recent national tragedies have indicated the degree to which community emergency services may be limited during a large-scale disaster. The CERT program is designed to equip local businesses or community organizations to be self-sustaining in such circumstances.

Though response teams are a valuable tool, there is risk associated with them. For example, workers on a volunteer internal fire brigade can be exposed to great risks when responding to a fire or chemical spill. You should evaluate applicable risks with appropriate legal counsel to determine if an internal team is the right tool for your organization.

INCIDENT INVESTIGATIONS

Workers can assist in investigating incidents. Those on the floor can be your greatest resource for information related to processes and procedures involved in incidents. They know how work should be done and can analyze the scene, providing unique input on what might have caused the incident.

Once causes have been identified, workers can be a great asset in determining what methods and procedures can be put in place to prevent recurrences. Being intimately familiar with work processes, they can make recommendations to improve the level of workplace safety.

Workers can accompany a supervisor or safety manager during an investigation. Confidentiality regarding certain issues must be exercised. Certain details may need to be filtered out of the information that you share with employees who are involved in an incident investigation. For example, medical records and workers' compensation information should not be openly shared. The focus should be on the incident, what caused it, and what can be done to prevent similar incidents in the future.

TASK OBSERVATIONS AND FEEDBACK

A behavior-based safety process can engage employees through conducting task observations. In this process, an employee uses a scripted form to conduct observations of coworkers while they perform certain tasks. The goal is to determine which behaviors may facilitate loss and which may prevent it. For example, an employee may be observed lifting a load properly, which prevents a back injury that could result in direct and indirect cost to your organization. Another employee might be observed not following standard operating procedures (SOP) for a piece of equipment. Violating the SOP could result in significant loss if an incident occurs.

Quantifying and evaluating data from these observations can point to strengths and weaknesses as indicated by employee behavior. Employees conducting these observations can provide immediate feedback. The observer and those who are being observed can discuss what took place and identify potential improvements or why it is important to follow established work protocols.

In a behavior-based process, it is important to avoid assuming that the behavior of a worker is solely driven by that worker. The behavior might actually be driven by a larger organizational system or the organizational culture. For example, an observation might occur and the worker is observed cutting a corner. The worker might explain that this deviation from proper procedure is a response to production demands. In other words, the corner-cutting behavior evolved as a way to satisfy management's production expectations. Though the worker made the decision to cut a corner, a larger issue is the organizational pressure that influenced that decision.

RECOMMENDATIONS

Any worker should feel free to make recommendations for preventing injuries or property damage. You should foster an organizational culture that allows the free flow of information between management and workers. Workers should feel comfortable approaching a member of management or a coworker to discuss a safety issue. Valuable and long-lasting change can result from it.

TIP LINES

Some workers may feel uncomfortable bringing an issue to management regardless of the culture that you have created. An employee may witness a coworker doing something that is unsafe but may feel uncomfortable reporting the event or may even feel threatened with reprisal if the coworker is confronted and penalized. A tip line or website can be set up for workers to report issues anonymously.

MAKE IT HAPPEN

Examine your organization and define ways in which workers can become involved in safety. Allow for a spectrum of activities that address the interests of your diverse workers, since not everyone wants to engage in the same type of activities. As workers become engaged in safety activities, you will need to provide them ongoing support and feedback.

Principle Five:
Lead Them

FROM THE STORY

Safety was not a significant part of the Axeon organizational culture, which resulted in little leadership being demonstrated in this area. Experiencing a fatality helped the leadership team to realize the importance of integrating safety into their operations and ways in which they could demonstrate safety leadership, such as the option Megan presented in the closing conference to include safety in preshift meetings.

■ ■ ■

A frequent quote used by the president of a university I attended was, "Everything rises and falls on leadership." When I first heard this, I believed that it was a bit simplistic and that a great deal of variables affects "everything" within a given organization. However, I have come to realize the truth of the statement as I have progressed through my career.

WORKER ENGAGEMENT

The theme of employee engagement is heavily represented in published research on leadership and leadership texts. This is also true in the specific area of workplace safety. The degree to which employees are involved can have a great impact on workplace safety performance.

Though we discussed the process of worker engagement fully in the previous principle, it is discussed here as a leadership methodology.

- **Employee commitment.** Engaging workers can result in their increased commitment to the organization (Petersen and Dotson, 2007). This can result in increased performance and a shared vision with organizational leaders. When leadership incorporates safety into personal behaviors, workers can begin to understand and become committed to creating a safe work environment and executing safe work behaviors.
- **Worker engagement without management abdicating responsibility.** Management must remain involved in safety in addition to engaging workers (Krause and Weekley, 2005). Continued management engagement helps avoid the perception that leaders are simply writing a check for safety when responding to worker requests for improvement. A strong relationship between engaged workers and managers held responsible for safety sets the stage for a productive environment in which safety can be improved and maintained in an authentic manner.
- **Worker role in problem-solving.** Leaders can engage workers in safety problem-solving (Peterson, 2004). Workers have specific knowledge due to their expertise in various daily tasks and therefore are appropriately positioned to provide alternatives in addressing risk of injury.
- **Relationships between management and workers.** Leaders must strive to maintain a positive relationship with workers in order for strong safety performance to occur (Cooper, 2001). I worked for two different organizations that had facilities in the same town. In the first, the facility struggled to improve in safety performance, while in the other, safety performance was very strong. When I joined the second organization, I expected to encounter similar problems as in the first, but instead, I found the environment quite different. I found this odd, because both facilities

hired from the same employment pool, paid similar wages, and provided similar working conditions. The one variable that was different was the relationship between employees and managers. At the first facility, it was strained, while at the second, it was very positive. A strong relationship between workers and managers can play a significant role in impacting safety performance.
- **Give employees control over their environment.** A collaborative opportunity for leaders and workers is to transition control over the environment to workers to increase safety performance (Geller, 2000). Rather than use a top-down system, providing employees with control over their environment in order to impact safety can increase worker commitment to the organization—and to safety in particular. Such an approach can help to build an environment of trust between leaders and workers where workers feel respected through being given a shared responsibility for safety.

ACCOUNTABILITY

Accountability for safety should take place on a number of levels. As with production and quality, leaders must hold individuals accountable for safety.

- **Leaders must hold others accountable.** Leaders should integrate safety as a point of accountability for both managers and workers (Geller, 2000). This can be accomplished through measuring safety performance at the departmental and shift levels so managers are aware of the safety performance within the scope of their responsibility. Workers can be held accountable through addressing at-risk behaviors that are exhibited while performing work. This makes workers aware that safety is a critical issue, and these behaviors are being observed by the leaders of the organization.
- **Managers must take responsibility for safety.** In addition to holding others accountable for safety, managers must take responsibility for safety (Simon & Frazee, 2005). Worker engagement in

safety must be balanced with managers taking responsibility for safety—workers should not perceive managers as abdicating this responsibility. Managers need to see themselves as holding a role that can have a direct influence on safety performance.
- **Employee self-accountability.** An evolution in safety is for workers to become self-accountable for safety (Geller, 2008). This is an optimal level of performance where workers take ownership of safety to the point where they reflect on their own work behavior and hold themselves accountable for safety before managers hold them accountable.

DEVELOP A CULTURE OF SAFETY

- **Safety correlates to success in business.** Though safety may be perceived as a necessary evil from a governmental compliance perspective, enhancing safety performance has a positive impact on overall business performance (Krause and Weekley, 2005). A fully developed and implemented health and safety management system can reduce work-related injuries, assisting in revenue-saving and revenue-generating activities such as reduced workers' compensation cost, quality of work (by keeping high-performing employees on the job), and increased reputation in the industry and in the eyes of the public. Imagine the financial loss that organizations suffer following explosions or other headline-grabbing incidents. A proactively safe environment where employees are involved can create an atmosphere where work is done correctly and without fear of injury and where they continually sense the care and support of organizational leaders.
- **Safety is not simply allocating money.** When only money is provided, workers do not sense a true commitment to workplace safety. They may perceive leaders as just throwing money at the problem rather than building a strong culture of safety. Instead, cultivate a culture of safety by involving leaders in safety

processes as well as spending on safety-improvement initiatives (Krause and Weekley, 2005).
- **Paradox between safety and production.** Workers may feel the constant battle between safety and production where a strong culture of safety is not present (Carillo, 2005). Safety must be so integrated into processes that safety is *how* work is conducted and not an appendage applied when convenient in times of low productivity. Safety must be woven into the organizational fabric so that workers perceive working safely as the way all work should be accomplished.
- **Workers must understand the culture**. A culture of safety can be developed so that workers are fully aware of it (Krause, 2004). This should be accomplished by design and not simply implied. The culture of safety should be designed so that workers are fully aware of safety efforts, such as leaders systematically engaging in safety communications, branding and symbols of safety being present in the workplace, and safety training workers receive on a routine basis. Designed manifestations of the culture of safety will help workers to understand the organization's culture and how it is demonstrated.
- **Organizations must define the culture.** Leaders can define and articulate the culture of safety to workers (Blair, 2003) so that they are fully aware of how it fits within the organizational culture. Defined traits can include open communication, safety symbols and branding, employee involvement, and training and education. Defining the safety component of the organizational culture can help leaders ensure that safety is developed as a cultural element and is monitored for growth.
- **The culture can be measured.** Similar to other aspects of organizational operations, the safety component of the organizational culture can be measured (Blair, 2003). Organizations routinely use employee-satisfaction surveys to measure how satisfied workers are with given aspects of their jobs, such as working conditions

and leadership. The concept of surveying employees can be applied to measuring the degree to which safety is being developed within the organizational culture. Workers can be asked an array of questions that address each aspect of safety cultural development as defined by the organization. Survey responses can help leaders to understand where safety is being effectively developed and where opportunities for improvement exist.

- **Safety is a value.** Safety should be seen as a value rather than simply as a priority (Cooper, 2001). If safety is being seen only as a priority, this may fuel the paradox workers can perceive between productivity and safety. An inherent issue is that priorities may change. Safety as a priority may slip to second place when production is perceived as the first priority, encouraging the paradox. Instead, safety should become a value within an organization so that it is nonnegotiable in how work is to be done. Production must be accomplished at a high level, but it must be done in a safe manner.
- **Safety efforts are encouraged and rewarded.** Along with other aspects of operations, efforts in the area of safety should be encouraged and rewarded among leaders and workers (Hansen, 2000). However, this must be done very thoughtfully. Safety incentive programs are a common initiative, but they may have undesired consequences. For example, if employees are rewarded for working a certain period of time without an injury, they may choose not to report a work-related injury to avoid losing the reward. On a leadership level, poorly designed safety incentive programs can lead to plant managers violating OSHA's recordkeeping standard by not properly recording injuries on the OSHA 300 log. To avoid these potential consequences, workers and managers should be rewarded for proactive activity that reduces the likelihood of injury. This can include rewards for participating on a safety committee or reporting safety hazards or near misses. Managers can be rewarded for things that are within their scope

of control, such as participating in safety inspections, assisting in incident investigations, or including safety topics in department or facility meetings.

SAFETY PROFESSIONAL RESPONSIBILITY

Leaders must effectively integrate into the organization any safety staffing that is in place.

- **Communicate to management.** Safety professionals must remain aware of regulatory and nonregulatory issues that must be addressed to develop a sufficient health and safety management system (Petersen & Dotson, 2007). Regulatory issues include local, state, and federal compliance requirements across a number of organizations such as OSHA, the Department of Transportation (DOT), and the National Fire Protection Association (NFPA). Safety professionals must navigate applicable requirements and work with management and workers to develop an implementation strategy. Safety professionals are also responsible to stay abreast of nonregulatory best practices, such as behavior-based safety, use of leading and lagging safety performance measures, prevention through design, and ergonomics. Nonregulatory issues should be considered in addition to basic regulatory requirements in building a robust safety management system.
- **Organization determines the degree of power.** Safety professionals are a tremendous asset in injury-reduction efforts, but the organization determines how much power they hold (Petersen, 2004). Bolman and Deal (2003) present the "human resource frame" that can be used to assess an organization to determine if it is properly structured. This frame can be used to determine if safety professionals are properly positioned for optimum effectiveness. For example, such an assessment can show whether safety professionals are positioned in the reporting structure with enough power to effect health and safety change and can

effectively communicate with decision-makers. It may be preferable for a safety manager to report to a plant manager, where direct safety communication can occur, as opposed to being at a secondary or tertiary levels where he or she is perceived as non-influential and has no direct access to the plant manager. Safety professionals should also be present on leadership teams typically composed of their peers in operations, maintenance, human resources, and finance and accounting. Membership on the leadership team can assist in elevating the importance of safety, having it formally recognized by managers and workers.

- **Measure safety performance.** Safety professionals must identify appropriate metrics to measure the performance of the safety management system (Krause, 2004). Metrics track both leading and lagging measures. Leading measures include quantifying proactive activities that impact injury reduction—for example, tracking the number of safety inspections, corrective measures, workplace safety observations, and safety topics covered in pre-shift meetings. Lagging measures quantify historical events—for example, tracking the number of injuries that have occurred, injury rate fluctuation, and workers' compensation cost. Lagging measures are typically used in organizations, but the challenge is that these measures only address failures. Integrating leading measures provides a more dynamic assessment of safety and health performance.

- **Establish worker and management measurements.** The safety professional can collaborate with human resources and organizational leaders to establish appropriate measures for workers and managers (Cooper, 2001). These measures should be well thought out and applied only to things that are within the individual's ability to achieve and can be integrated into the performance evaluation system. For example, it is difficult to apply a general percentage of injury reduction in a department to a department manager. Instead, the manager could be held accountable for individual

actions that influence the percentage of reduction, such as the number of safety inspections conducted, safety topics covered in preshift meetings, and corrective measures implemented. These are things over which a manager holds personal control.
- **Correlate injury-reduction efforts with operational goals.** Safety professionals can connect the impact of injury reduction efforts to achieving operational goals (Hansen, 2000). Communicating this connection can foster ongoing support for injury reduction efforts. For example, a reduction in lost-time injuries results in high-performing workers staying in their typical work positions instead of being injured and placed off of work and forcing the use of a less-experienced worker in a role where quality problems could arise or production thresholds may not be achieved. A reduction in injuries can impact an organization's ability to keep healthy, high-performing workers on the job.

MANAGEMENT ENGAGEMENT

Management must exhibit active engagement in order for a safety management system to develop and have a maximum amount of impact. As workers observe managers becoming involved, they will begin to accept safety as a true component of the organizational culture.

- **Take responsibility for failure.** When injuries occur, the associated managers must take responsibility for what occurred (Geller, 2008). They need to acknowledge things over which they had control that led to the injury. This realization will help managers to improve in areas where they can impact safety. A concept that can improve the process of taking responsibility is the avoidance of blame or faultfinding. In an injury investigation an error that can be made is to simply place blame rather than working to find the root causes of the incident and implement corrective action. When blame is sought, a temptation might be to improperly place fault on a worker who may have demonstrated behavior that was the direct catalyst for the injury. Doing so can cause managers to miss all of the other facilitating factors that led to the injury, thus shifting blame away from the manager and onto the worker. Managers can have a great deal of influence on causes of injuries. Activities such as placing stress on workers and not enforcing safety procedures can cause workers to adopt unsafe work practices that lead to injury. Managers can reflect on their role in an injury, take responsibility as appropriate, and implement corrective behavior to prevent future injuries.

- **Managers focus on core issues that affect business growth.** In daily operations, managers address issues within their scope of responsibility that have an impact on business growth (Petersen & Dotson, 2007). They may be measured on such things as production and quality and will focus on improvement in these areas because they know they are being monitored to improve business growth. Safety needs to be integrated as an area of business growth. Organizations with high safety performance enjoy strong overall performance (Krause and Weekley, 2005). Including safety in an organization at the same level of business concerns such as production and quality can result in managers focusing on safety improvement as a key element of organizational success.

- **Only senior management can instill safety as a value.** Senior management is in a uniquely powerful position to instill safety as a value in an organization (Petersen and Dotson, 2007). Safety should become a value in how work is accomplished rather than simply a priority, where it might be lost in the fray in periods of high and fast-paced production. Instilling safety as a value starts with leaders. They must incorporate safety as a visible component of organizational activity.

- **Behavior and commitment are predictors of success in safety.** Leaders who actively demonstrate safety behavior and commitment can have a direct impact on safety improvement (Krause and Weekley, 2005). If workers are expected to buy into safety, they must first see it demonstrated by leaders. When the work environment requires safety-toe shoes and safety glasses, but workers see leaders walk into the plant without such personal protective equipment, they may question the authenticity of safety efforts. Leaders must have a personal commitment to safety and manifest it through behavior consistent with that commitment.

- **Key involvement of safety in other organizational activities.** Leaders can strive to improve safety through making safety a key component of organizational activities (Simon and Frazee, 2005). Rather than address safety only in safety training sessions or during times of safety recognition, leaders can include safety as a component of other activities, such as plant meetings and quarterly business reviews. When safety is included in these activities, it can be seen as a significant component of the organization and something that leaders care about.
- **Engage in safety always—not just in response to an incident.** Unfortunately, leaders sometimes become involved in safety only when an incident occurs (Carillo, 2005). This can change when leaders become aware of safety hazards that impact their workforce and take the appropriate steps to correct problems before an injury occurs. Leaders can also become aware of the benefit of safety to the success of the organization and include safety in routine activities and meetings so it becomes an integral part of business operations.
- **Create culture**. Leaders are in a powerful position to drive the creation of organizational culture (Blair, 2003). They can take advantage of this opportunity by moving safety beyond just a priority to a value and key component integrated within the organizational culture.
- **Establish a vision of safety excellence.** Leaders have the opportunity to instill a vision of safety excellence for their organizations (Cooper, 2001). Kotter (1996) supports the idea of leaders setting

the vision for an organization. Senior management should include safety in this vision, which can in turn instill safety as an organizational value. Integrate safety in the vision by incorporating it as a component of the mission statement and then in key communications throughout the year. The presence of safety in such communications can help everyone in the organization to understand the important of safety.

MAKE IT HAPPEN

Safety leadership must be situated in all levels of management from department managers to CEOs. Opportunities for safety leadership should be identified and executed by all leaders within the organization. Workers perceive what their organizational leaders say and do as important, so leaders can significantly impact safety performance by including safety in appropriate meetings and demonstrating safe work behavior. There are practical ways in which industry leaders can demonstrate safety leadership. They can:

- **Engage in safety activities**
    - *Assist in conducting safety inspections.* Accompany a worker, manager, or safety professional on an inspection. It could be an isolated forklift pre-use inspection requiring little time up to a full facility inspection that may require a few hours.
    - *Attend a safety committee meeting.* Your presence at a monthly safety committee meeting demonstrates support for safety and allows you to hear what workers are thinking regarding safety.
    - *Be present during worker safety training.* A few words from you at the start of a safety training session sends a clear message to workers that safety is an important component of how work is done. Staying for the training session and even participating in it can forge stronger ties to workers when they see your willingness to understand the work they perform.

- **Hold managers and workers accountable for safety**
    - *Include safety in annual performance evaluations.* Evaluate workers on individually achievable safety performance objectives. For example, stipulating a 10 percent reduction in injuries as a metric for a departmental manager's success is not feasible, because the manager cannot control the behavior of all department workers him- or herself. However, the manager can accomplish things that influence the desired 10 percent reduction, such as conducting safety tours of work areas, including safety in preshift meetings and ensuring all employees have received needed safety training. Activities such as these can be measured and are within the ability of the department manager to accomplish as an individual.
    - *Engage human resources corrective action procedures equitably.* When unsafe acts occur that result in injury or property damage, both managers and workers should be held accountable through applicable human resources corrective action processes. Treat every individual in the same, equitable manner when walking through corrective action procedures.
- **Include safety in organizational meetings**
    - Departmental preshift or toolbox meetings can serve as a daily or periodic avenue through which safety information can be shared. Communicate safety information in a short and concise manner while providing ongoing emphasis on safety over time.
    - Periodic facility meetings can include applicable safety information, such as key risks that might need to be addressed or safety performance measures. Workers perceive as important what they hear in such meetings. If safety is included, it will help them understand the degree of importance being placed on their protection.
    - Leadership team meetings allow safety to be discussed on a strategic level. Safety performance measures can be discussed

as well as how safety is assisting in improving operations. The safety manager/director should be included on such teams to give safety direct visibility to all members of facility or organizational leadership.
- o Quarterly business reviews that include higher-level executives are opportunities to discuss safety at the organizational level. Discuss safety initiatives and performance based on reports from facilities or business units throughout the organization.
- o Annual business reports can communicate macrolevel safety performance data and identify how various facilities or business units have performed compared to goals and percentage of improvement or decline from the previous fiscal year.

- **Include safety in organizational goals**
  - o *Ensure that safety goals are appropriate and achievable.* A fallacy in many formal safety goal-setting agendas is that the target should be zero injuries. Though this is understandable from a moral perspective, it can have negative indirect outcomes because *zero* implies perfection, which is very difficult to achieve, let alone maintain. A facility where someone suffers an injury early in the fiscal year may lower safety efforts because it has already missed the annual goal of zero injuries. A better approach is to identify a realistic percentage of reduction in injury rate.
  - o *Define a clear strategy to accomplish each safety goal.* Define no more than three or four tangible activities for achieving each safety goal. One goal might be to reduce injuries by 10 percent. Strategies to accomplish it could include conducting applicable safety training for all employees, conducting risk assessments on work tasks to ensure that risks to injury and fatality are being properly managed, and implementing a safety inspection process.

Oregon OSHA (2011b) also delineated ways in which industry leaders can demonstrate an ongoing commitment to protecting workers:

- *Write a company safety policy.* Such a high-level document can be one page that clearly communicates the integration of safety into organizational operations and work-performance expectations.
- *Have leaders set the safety example.* Make sure that workers follow safe work practices by having leaders set the example. That way, workers accept safety as an authentic component of the organization.
- *Give workers the authority they need to carry out their safety responsibilities.* Workers should be given the latitude to report and immediately address safety issues observed in the work environment.
- *Budget the time and resources to achieve workplace safety goals.* Safety should receive equal attention as all other operational areas in annual budgets. Budgets should address the financial, physical, and human resources needed to manage and lead safety effectively.
- *Act on recommendations from the safety committee or individual employees.* Follow through on the identification of safety issues is critical. Workers need to see the correction of safety deficiencies and the improvement of work processes to perceive an emphasis on their protection as legitimate.
- *Make sure workers have the safety and health training they need to do their jobs.* Some safety issues are basic, while others are complex. Training employees on housekeeping issues takes a relatively short time, while training them on permit-required confined space entry is much more complex and time intensive. Leaders need to provide opportunities and the time and resources for workers to be properly trained so they can perform their jobs safely.

Principle Six:
Find It and Fix It

FROM THE STORY

Axeon managed the identification and elimination of hazards in the work environment reactively, responding to a string of minor incidents. The leadership team had been lulled into a false sense of security, believing that no significant risks to worker safety existed because only minor injuries had occurred so far. It took a fatality for its members to view their work environment differently. Integrating a safety manager into the leadership team and engaging workers were first steps toward proactively building a safety-management system in which hazards would be identified and addressed before another injury or fatality occurred.

■ ■ ■

To protect workers, you must first find the things in your work environment that can cause them injury. Risk assessments identify risks to workers and help you to prioritize what areas to focus on based on levels of risk. You will be aware of what risks are present and also their levels in relation to the severity of potential injury.

A risk assessment involves observing and analyzing a job as it is performed to determine the probability and severity of an injury occurring from different exposures to risks as the job is performed. Conducting risk assessments will benefit your organization in a number of ways:

- Injuries will be prevented as you gain an understanding of what risks are present and how to protect workers from them.
- Documented risk assessments help you create safe work procedures.
- Your bottom line will be strengthened due to reduced direct and indirect cost related to accidents, since jobs will be performed safely based on information gained in the risk assessment process.
- Productivity will increase as workers are healthy and safe.
- Documented risk assessments can be used as a training tool to teach new or transferred workers how to properly perform tasks.

WHERE TO START

Conducting risk assessments can be a significant undertaking, depending on the size and complexity of the work being done within a given organization. Constructive ways to begin moving through the process include:

- *Talk with and involve workers in the risk assessment process.* First, speaking with workers can help identify some of the hazards in the workplace that cause them concern. These hazards can serve as a starting point in the risk assessment process. Second, workers can be involved in conducting risk assessments. With proper training, they can assist in observing work as it is being performed, identifying hazards to which workers are exposed, and determining the appropriate responses to protect workers effectively.
- *Review incident records to determine what hazards are resulting in worker injuries.* Incident investigation forms should provide details of the causes of any injuries. This can guide you on where to focus your initial risk assessment efforts.

- As resources allow, the goal should be to conduct risk assessments on all jobs. Plan to implement such a program over a longer period so that you can assess each job.

ADDRESSING HAZARDS

Once a risk assessment has been conducted and hazards have been identified, the appropriate control method needs to be determined. Though various models exist, fundamental control methods include, in order of preference:

- **Avoidance.** Prevent introducing the risk of worker injury when you first design work processes.
- **Substitution.** Replace an item or process that results in a hazard, such as replacing a hazardous chemical with a safer alternative.
- **Engineering.** Physically improve the work environment, such as installing a guard that covers a moving part on a machine that could result in a worker's body part being pinched or cut.
- **Administration.** Manage work processes to control risk of injury, such as using job rotation to lessen exposure to strains or sprains that can occur through repetitive motion.
- **Personal protective equipment.** Provide workers with fall protection equipment where they are exposed to falls, or gloves where they might be exposed to cuts or puncture wounds.

Avoidance, substitution, and engineering controls are preferable since they are more effective in fully removing the risk of injury. Administrative and personal protective equipment controls are useful in lessening exposure to workplace hazards, but they introduce the element of human error. For example, if personal protective equipment is the selected control, workers must still remember to wear and maintain it properly. The preference is to remove a risk in some way rather than manage it in place.

AUDIT THE PROCESS
Conducting risk assessments is not a one-time event. Risk assessments should be reviewed periodically to ensure that appropriate safeguards are in place to protect workers. A periodic review process is important because:

- **Jobs change.** Work processes and procedures may change over time, which could result in new risks being introduced into the workplace.
- **Products change.** Product ingredients may change, resulting in a need to review any hazards a new substance may present.
- **Equipment changes.** Facility improvements might include the introduction of new or refurbished equipment, possibly introducing new hazards.
- **People change.** Numerous human factors mean that risk assessments must be revisited to determine if any change in risk has occurred. Such factors could include an aging workforce, non-English-speaking workers, young workers, or a rate of turnover that introduces an influx of inexperienced workers.

MAKE IT HAPPEN
A risk assessment process can be implemented by addressing worker and management responsibilities:

- **Workers**
    - *Workers must receive training on hazard identification.* You cannot assume that workers are naturally aware of hazards in the workplace. Workers must be educated on things that can result in injury. Individual workers may have developed an internal level of risk tolerance that might need to be overcome.
    - *Your safety program must require workers to report hazards.* Workers are intimately familiar with all operational issues and are best positioned to identify hazards in the workplace that

must be addressed. Hazard reporting can be carried out through stipulated mechanisms, such as reporting them to a:
- Coworker, to address immediate exposure to a hazard
- Manager, to initiate a long-term solution for controlling the hazard
- Safety committee, who works with management to ensure safe, ongoing management of the hazard

- **Management**
  - Must receive training on hazard identification and risk assessment
  - Must use their training to direct the hazard reporting process and follow up to ensure that hazards are being safely controlled
  - Upper management needs to provide resources to address hazards, which could include:
    - Financial: a budget for addressing identified hazards
    - Personnel: if not present, safety professionals may need to be staffed to lead risk assessment efforts
    - Equipment: certain equipment might be needed to adequately assess the level of risk, such as exposure monitoring equipment

A proactive tool that can be used is the process of prevention through design (ANSI/ASSE Z590.3). Prevention through design includes a consideration of workplace safety in the design phase of new construction or facility renovations. Discussing workplace safety issues and risk assessment and control in the early stages of construction or renovation promotes a safer work environment from the outset rather than the prospect of costly retrofits once construction is complete and plant operations begin.

Principle Seven:
Measure It

FROM THE STORY

Measurement of safety performance had not been a part of the management system at Axeon Logistics. Though other areas of the business had been closely monitored through such communications as profit-and-loss statements, safety performance measurement had not been part of the process. Guy and the rest of the leadership team later realized the need to include a system that accounted for both leading and lagging measures of safety.

■ ■ ■

A safety and health management system includes written programs that direct your effort, defines leadership activities, provides opportunities for worker engagement, and trains workers on how to perform their jobs safely. Once you establish your system, you must measure how well it functions by using leading and lagging measures. Blair and O'Toole (2010, p. 29) stated, "The problem many organizations encounter is that the measures they use do not provide adequate feedback for continuous improvement of the safety process nor do they contribute to the development of the safety culture." Organizations must evaluate the unique aspects of safety that impact their workplaces and define both leading and lagging measures that will help to shape opportunities for improvement, and they must then take the necessary actions to fully protect workers.

LEADING MEASURES

Leading measures help you to quantify proactive events that promote strong safety performance. For example, you may conduct inspections that result in corrective action to address the safety issues that were identified. Housekeeping inspections, for example, prevent basic slips, trips, and falls, which remain a significant problem in many workplaces and result in injuries and associated direct and indirect costs. Daily housekeeping inspections can be used to proactively observe workplaces to ensure hazards are identified and addressed. Responses may be short term or long term:

- **Short term.** Debris found during a housekeeping inspection can be immediately removed and properly disposed of.
- **Long term.** If subsequent housekeeping inspections reveal continuing collection of debris, the housekeeping program and worker training may need to be examined to identify where they can be improved to address the issue systemically.

Organizations can explore, evaluate, and select leading measures that are most appropriate. Examples of leading measures that could be useful for an organization include:

- **Behavioral observations.** Observing work processes allows you to quantify safe and at-risk behavior. You can create a checklist of necessary behaviors for a job to be performed safely. For example, a job might require personal protective equipment, which includes a hard hat, safety glasses, leather gloves, and safety-toe boots. A particular observation of someone on the job may reveal that all PPE was properly worn except gloves. This would translate into a metric of the job being performed 75 percent safe in relation to PPE (three safe behaviors executed divided by four safe behaviors desired). The checklist could include additional safe behaviors, such as following specified safe work procedures, communicating effectively with coworkers in the area, and proper body positioning (ergonomics). Goals could be set for a certain number of behavioral observations to collect data that can then be acted on to increase the level of safety in the workplace.

- **Safety committee activities.** Safety committee activities can be quantified to determine how active the safety committee is and what impact its work has on safety performance. For example, data could be collected and analyzed on the volume and quality of recommendations that safety committee members make or are reported to it. Data could also be collected and analyzed on safety improvements made as a result of the recommendations.
- **Safety improvements.** Beyond work done specifically by a safety committee (or in the absence of a safety committee), you may collect and analyze data on safety reports or recommendations made to management and any improvements that result.
- **Near-miss reports.** Workers should be encouraged to report near misses, which are incidents where the stage was set for an accident to occur, but there was no actual injury or property damage. For example, a forklift operator transporting a load through a warehouse might narrowly miss a pedestrian in a congested area. Information from near-miss reports can be collected and analyzed to determine possible trends, and action can then be taken to avoid future incidents. Collecting near-miss reports over time may reveal other similar near misses involving forklifts and pedestrians and lead to a reorganization of the work environment to lessen congestion and retraining of forklift operators to use their horns and to be vigilant and yield to pedestrians.
- **Training sessions.** Communicating hazards and preventive measures to workers can assist in reducing worker injuries and associated costs. Workers who have been properly trained know

about workplace hazards and how to perform their jobs safely. Measuring the number of safety training sessions can serve as one metric, but you should also measure the quality of the training to ensure that it meets the needs of workers and the organization.

LAGGING MEASURES

Lagging measures quantify past incidents and can help you to identify trends that must be addressed. Such measures have been used historically when assessing safety performance and include:

- **OSHA injury rates.** Injury rates are calculated using the formula:

    (number of injuries x 200,000) / number of hours worked

    Two hundred thousand is a constant in the formula, representing one hundred workers who work forty hours per week for fifty weeks per year (two weeks are estimated for vacation and holidays). For a given year in which a facility experienced fifteen OSHA recordable injuries and a total of two million hours among all workers and managers, the OSHA recordable rate would then be calculated as (15 x 200,000) / 2,000,000 = 1.5. This result indicates that 1.5 workers experienced an OSHA-recordable injury for every one hundred workers at the facility. The rate is useful in evaluating year-to-year safety performance since it provides a somewhat reliable measurement regardless of the exact number of hours worked in a given year. In addition to examining the OSHA recordable rate, other rates could be evaluated, such as that of restricted work incidents (when workers cannot perform their standard jobs due to injury and are placed in a restricted work assignment during the healing process), lost-time incidents (when workers must remain at home for at least one day to recover from an injury), and fatalities.

- **Number of injuries.** The number of injuries alone can be used as a lagging measurement but may not be accurate because of fluctuation in hours worked.
- **Workers' compensation cost.** The financial impact of each injury can be measured to find the direct cost of the current level of safety performance. Such cost typically includes medical costs, workers' compensation payments made to an employee, and the cost to the organization to manage the claim, such as attorney fees or the use of experts in investigating the claim.
- **Indirect cost.** Indirect cost of an injury is hard-to-capture data, such as the loss of quality or production that may result from injury. Research indicates that for every dollar of injury-related direct cost (workers' compensation cost), an organization might suffer an additional loss of $2 to $4, making indirect cost a much greater portion of financial loss due to poor safety performance (National Safety Council, 2013). In other words, if a facility has spent $200,000 in direct cost to manage injuries, the additional indirect cost could be as much as $800,000, resulting in a total expense of $1 million due to work-related injuries.

SAFETY MANAGEMENT SYSTEM AUDITS

Organizations routinely conduct financial audits. Similarly, safety management system auditing can help you assess how well the safety management system is functioning. Safety auditing is a leading measure process by which programs are evaluated to determine their effectiveness and level of compliance. Auditing can be utilized in three areas:

- Program start-up audits
- Annual system audits
- Targeted audits

PROGRAM START-UP AUDITS

Shortly after implementing a new compliance program, such as a fall protection program, it is beneficial to audit each aspect of the program and make immediate corrections if needed. The best-laid plans may still have problems once they are implemented. Even when you assemble a good team with a proper variety of personnel to create a program, it can be difficult to plan for every contingency. You may need to perform a preliminary audit of the program's effectiveness within ninety days of implementation, a period that provides enough time for the program to begin working and for potential problems or successes to surface.

ANNUAL SYSTEM AUDITS

Once you have a safety and health management system that includes a comprehensive scope of safety programs that address all hazards in the workplace, it is important to periodically review the system to ensure that it is up-to-date, functioning properly, and is relevant to the hazards and personnel involved. Do this at least annually. Such an evaluation gives you a fresh look at the program and helps you to determine if revisions are necessary.

The auditing process includes three areas of evaluation of your safety management system:

- Documentation review
- Facility inspection
- Worker and management interviews

DOCUMENTATION REVIEW

The primary reason to implement a safety program is that it is the right thing to do for an employer to invest time, money, and other resources to provide a safe work environment for each employee. However, compliance to legal requirements is also necessary. OSHA provides basic requirements for safety and health issues in the Code of Federal Regulations. At a minimum, each component of a safety program that is affected by a specific regulation should be audited on a scheduled interval to ensure that the company is satisfying regulatory requirements.

Documents to be reviewed during a safety system audit include the base written programs or policies and all documentation used to implement them. The programs or policies should be evaluated to determine that they address all of the pertinent issues within the scope of the topic being addressed. Typically, this includes an evaluation of the stated purpose of the program or policy, delineation of responsibilities, written safe work procedures, worker and management training content, and statement of internal periodic program or policy review. Supporting documentation review includes an evaluation of records such as training documentation, work permits, emergency contact lists, risk assessments, completed incident investigation forms, and completed inspection forms.

Safety policies and procedures maintained on file or in policy manuals should remain applicable to current worker positions within an organization. As a business changes, it may be necessary to add new programs, revise current programs, or remove information that no longer applies to the workforce.

FACILITY INSPECTION

A completed documentation review provides an understanding of what the facility management states is being done within the safety management system. A facility inspection provides the first step in understanding how well the safety management system is actually being executed. Such an inspection includes a tour of every part of the facility, thorough observation of every aspect of the operation, including work as it is being done, and the physical state of the facility. The goal is to ensure that the facility is physically conducive to providing safety for all workers and managers.

WORKER AND MANAGEMENT INTERVIEWS

Training is a critical area OSHA focuses on during worker interviews during compliance inspections. The level of success of training you offer is shown by how well workers can respond to questions and demonstrate training they have received. For example, if a worker has been trained in the use of dry chemical fire extinguishers, he or she should be able to converse easily on the topic and demonstrate their use. Ask your workers questions about safety training they have already received to verify that they understand and can apply the material.

AUDITORS

Safety audits may be conducted by a variety of individuals within an organization. If a company employs a full-time safety manager, the temptation is to relegate this responsibility to him or her. A safety manager should be an effective auditor, but auditing should be a tool to involve other members of management and, in some situations, hourly workers. Allowing different personnel to perform safety program audits will help them to take a greater level of ownership of the program. Those chosen to perform audits should be selected with legal liability in mind: an auditor may need access to confidential information. In this case, a member of management may have to fill the role. An auditor must also possess sufficient knowledge and skill to adequately evaluate safety issues.

SAFETY-SYSTEM-AUDIT MEASUREMENT

Each section of the audit should be scored, as should the audit as a whole. An audit can be conducted without scoring, but it will be of no use to measure year-to-year improvement if only a list of deficiencies is generated. Audit scoring can measure a number of areas of organizational performance:

- Use isolated scores for the documentation review, facility inspection, and worker and management interviews to identify phases of the implementation process that might need specific attention.
- Use isolated scores for each audit topic, such as fall protection, across the documentation review, facility inspection, and worker and management interview sections to identify parts of the safety management system that might need attention.
- A score for the audit as a whole provides a metric indicating the level of the safety-management system's performance.

There are two primary audit scoring strategies to present the level of safety performance:

- **Yes/no assessment.** A yes/no scoring methodology simply indicates whether items are satisfactory or unsatisfactory. For example, a yes response to a question such as, "Are all emergency exits clear of obstruction?" indicates a favorable condition. A challenge with this methodology is that no responses can skew the true picture of what is occurring at a facility. If a facility has twenty emergency exits and two are blocked, the auditor may assess a no response due to all exits not being clear, when the reality is that 90 percent of the exits are actually being maintained properly.
- **Graduated assessment.** Graduated scoring can include a range of assessment options that provide a more granular understanding of safety performance. Options could include a range of scores from 0 to 3 or a similar ranking where 0 indicates no compliance, 1 indicates some compliance with significant issues, 2 indicates a great deal of compliance with minor issues, and 4 indicates complete compliance. In the previous emergency exit example, 3 might be assessed because most emergency exits are in compliance. Audit scoring utilizing this methodology generates more specific data, which helps you to better understand the status of the safety management system.

SAFETY SYSTEM AUDIT RESPONSE

Certain items that are immediately dangerous to life or health (IDLH) must be fixed during the audit, such as workers who are witnessed by the auditor as working where there is an exposure to a fall. General findings from the audit should be prioritized by risk level category of the potential for injury. One way to categorize findings for follow-up and corrective action is by:

- High risk: must be addressed within twenty-four hours
- Moderate risk: must be addressed within thirty days
- Low risk: must be addressed within ninety days

The auditor can indicate within the document the category into which each finding is assessed. The auditor can also work with management and workers throughout the year following the audit to ensure each deficiency is addressed appropriately and in a timely manner.

TARGETED AUDITS

Components of the annual safety system audit can address specific issues of concern. For example, if behavioral observation or incident investigation data indicates a recurring trend of problems related to the use of fall protection, a targeted audit document can be developed that specifically addresses fall protection. This type of streamlined audit can quickly capture data and pinpoint problems. Similar to the safety system audit, a targeted audit can include a review of the fall protection program, records associated with its implementation, a facility inspection in which observations are made of all tasks involving fall protection, and worker and management interviews. The audit can be scored, giving an understanding of specifically where problems with the program exist. Corrective action can then be taken to address problem areas.

INSPECTIONS

Although inspections are typically used to identify deficiencies, they can integrate quantitative data collection to be used as a leading measure of safety performance. Inspections can be conducted in different areas and at different intervals, such as:

- Daily forklift pre-use inspections
- Weekly housekeeping inspections
- Monthly fire extinguisher or safety inspections
- Quarterly fire system inspections

Inspection documents can be used to generate data by simply tabulating a percentage of favorable findings compared to the total number of items being inspected. For example, a daily forklift inspection process might be in place and appears to be functioning well. Inspections are being conducted, and maintenance is responding to identified repair issues. However, if the inspection is converted to a data collection tool, analysis could reveal the volume and type of issues that are being addressed. Rather than continue to respond merely to equipment failures, effort could be more productively placed in the preventive maintenance program so that failures are avoided in the first place. Such activity could result in better equipment utilization as well as saving significant money with investment in preventive maintenance instead of repairs generated by running equipment to the point of failure.

MAKE IT HAPPEN

Identifying the appropriate safety system measurements is a unique task for each organization. The challenge is to identify a system of measurements that can be most readily understood by managers and workers and have the greatest impact in assessing and addressing safety performance. You can engage workers and managers in developing the measures that are most appropriate for your organization.

If you are just beginning the process, it might be advisable to start small and work toward a larger system of measurement. You could begin with isolating the areas of your greatest safety risks by developing targeted audits and then build over time toward a more robust system that captures a comprehensive scope of measurements, including a safety management system audit.

If you have safety measurements in place, now could be a time to revisit your system to ensure that the measurements you have in place are meaningful in impacting safety performance. Lagging measures might be a mainstay of your measurement processes, and there could be opportunity to integrate leading measures that will allow you to identify issues and take corrective action before an incident occurs.

Applying the Seven Principles

You might feel overwhelmed now and think, *There is so much we need to do. I have no idea where to start!* Or you might be thinking, *We are already doing all of this. We're in good shape.* Or you might be resting somewhere between these two extremes, realizing where you have opportunity for improvement.

If you feel overwhelmed or have accomplished work in safety with more to do, there is always a light at the end of the tunnel. You might have a lot of work to do, but you can relax, knowing that you do not have to tackle all of the principles at once. The principles are designed to provide you with a framework that can help lead you to more fully protecting your most valuable asset: your workers. As with any journey, you simply need to take the first step. Individually or with a leadership team, reflect on the seven principles and determine which one or two of them might represent a logical beginning for your journey. The principles do not need to be explored sequentially as presented here. You can navigate each principle and determine along the way where you need to make an immediate impact based on the risks in your workplace and considering the unique attributes of your organizational culture. By taking one step at a time, you can work toward building a robust safety management system.

If you believe you are already executing each of the seven principles, now might be a time to analyze your organization and reflect on how well you are actually doing in regard to each principle. Such a process might lead to enlightenment and discovery, where you realize that although you are doing good work in relation to each of the principles, opportunity exists for continuous improvement. For example, you might find that you are engaging workers in safety, but there are additional ways in which you can build on that foundation and strengthen worker engagement and the resulting relationship between workers and management.

A deep exploration using the seven principles can help you design or improve on a safety and health management that can lead to greater organizational performance and worker safety. If you truly believe that workers are your most valuable asset, what you do to build a functioning and effective safety management system will help them see the evidence of your commitment behind your words.

Charting Your Course

One way to use this book is within a management team, safety committee, or other organizational team discussion group. Teams can meet periodically to discuss sections of the book and generate ideas for safety improvement. Following are discussion questions related to each principle that you can use as a guide for discussion when you begin charting your course or possibly to make improvements on the direction you are already traveling.

PRINCIPLE ONE: IT MAKES BUSINESS SENSE

- How are we tracking costs related to safety incidents?
- How are we determining direct costs?
- How are we determining indirect costs?
- How are we determining our return on investment in safety expenditures?
- What methods should we use to communicate financial information related to safety?
- Who should receive this information?
- What methods should we use to better integrate safety into business financial data?

PRINCIPLE TWO: COMPLY

- What compliance programs do we currently have in place?
- What compliance gaps exist?
- Who is responsible for various aspects of ongoing compliance?
- Are responsibilities appropriately distributed among the right people in our organization? If not, in what way could we improve?
- What implementation tools could be improved upon?
- What program implementation challenges have we experienced?
- How can we learn from challenges to ensure future success?

PRINCIPLE THREE: TEACH THEM

- What methods are we currently using to train workers and managers?
- What other training methods might be more effective in ensuring learning?
- How can we better address the varied learning needs of our workers?
- Have we provided sufficient time for training? If not, how can we better manage our time?
- How do we know workers have learned what we believe we have taught them?

PRINCIPLE FOUR: ENGAGE THEM

- What ways exist for workers and managers to be engaged in safety?
- What opportunities for engagement could we add to our current list of opportunities?
- If we have a safety committee, is it properly structured and organized? What value have we experienced from the safety committee? How might the safety committee improve?
- In what ways has management responded to recommendations made by workers as a result of worker engagement in safety?
- In what ways can management encourage workers to become more engaged in safety?
- In what ways does our organizational culture encourage or discourage worker engagement in safety?

PRINCIPLE FIVE: LEAD THEM

- In what ways does senior management demonstrate leadership in safety?
- In what ways do other members of management demonstrate leadership in safety?

- How do workers respond to current leadership efforts?
- In what ways can we improve the ways in which we lead safety?
- Has organizational leadership properly positioned safety staff within the organizational structure for maximum impact?

PRINCIPLE SIX: FIND IT AND FIX IT

- How are we identifying risks to worker injury?
- How are workers and managers being equipped to identify risks?
- What processes do we have in place to address risks that have been identified?
- What opportunities exist for improving the way we address risks of worker injury?

PRINCIPLE SEVEN: MEASURE IT

- What lagging measures are we using to determine our level of safety performance?
- What lagging measures should we add to our existing list?
- What leading measures are we using to determine our level of safety performance?
- What leading measures should we add to our existing list?
- How are we using auditing as a form of measurement of our safety management system?
- Is our audit scoring system providing us with as much detail as possible? If not, how should we adjust our audit scoring methodology?
- In what ways can we improve our auditing process?
- How should we communicate the results of our measurement throughout the organization? What methods should we use, and who should receive information from the various forms of measurement?

References

Blair, E. 2003. "Culture & Leadership: Seven Key Points for Improved Safety Performance." *Professional Safety* 48 (6): 18–22.

Blair, E., and M. O'Toole. 2010. "Leading Measures: Enhancing Safety Climate and Driving Safety Performance." *Professional Safety* 55 (8): 29–34.

Bolman, L., and T. Deal. 2001. *Leading with Soul: An Uncommon Journey of Spirit*. San Francisco: Jossey-Bass.

———. 2003. *Reframing Organizations: Artistry, Choice and Leadership*. San Francisco: Jossey-Bass.

Bureau of Labor Statistics. 2016a. "All Charts, Census of Fatal Occupational Injuries." Accessed April 24, 2017, https://www.bls.gov/iif/oshcfoi1.htm#2015.

———. 2016b. "Numbers of Non-fatal Occupational Injuries and Illnesses by Industry and Case Types, 2015." Accessed April 24, 2017, https://www.bls.gov/iif/oshwc/osh/os/ostb4734.pdf.

Carillo, R. 2005. "Safety Leadership: Managing the Paradox." *Professional Safety* 50 (7): 31–34.

Cekada, T. 2012. "Training a Multigenerational Workforce." *Professional Safety* 57 (3): 40–44.

Cooper, D. 2001. "Treating Safety as a Value." *Professional Safety* 46 (2): 17–21.

Cullen, E. T. 2008. "Tell Me a Story: Using Stories to Improve Occupational Safety Training." *Professional Safety* 53 (7): 20–27.

Deming, W. E. "Deming's 1950 lecture to Japanese management." Accessed April 24, 2017, http://hclectures.blogspot.com/1970/08/demings-1950-lecture-to-japanese.html.

Dunlap, S., B. Dudak, and M. Konty. 2012. "Adult Education in Higher Education: A Synthesized Model for Integrating Principles of Adult Learning in the Higher Education Classroom." *Kentucky Journal of Excellence in College Teaching and Learning* (Fall): 19–35.

EHS Today. "Agreement with U.S. Department of Justice Gives Bite to OSHA's Bark in Criminal Cases." Accessed April 24, 2017, http://ehstoday.com/osha/agreement-us-department-justice-gives-bite-osha-s-bark-criminal-cases.

Elias, J., and S. Merriam. 2000. *Philosophical Foundations of Adult Education*, 3rd ed. Malabar, FL: Krieger.

Geller, S. 2000. "10 Leadership Qualities for a Total Safety Culture: Safety Management Is Not Enough." *Professional Safety* 45 (5): 38–41.

———. 2008. "People-based Leadership: Enriching a Work Culture for World-class Safety." *Professional Safety* 53 (3): 29–36.

Hansen, L. 2000. "The Architecture of Safety Excellence." *Professional Safety* 45 (5): 26–29.

Jennings, K., and J. Stahl-Wert. 2005. *The Serving Leader: 5 Powerful Actions That Will Transform Your Team, Your Business and Your Community*. San Francisco: Berrett-Koehler Publishers.

Kotter, J. 1996 *Leading Change*. Boston: Harvard Business School Press.

Krause, T. 2004 "Influencing the Behavior of Senior Leadership: What Makes a Great Safety Leader?" *Professional Safety* 49 (6): 29–33.

Krause, T., and T. Weekley. 2005. "Safety Leadership: A Four-factor Model for Establishing a High-functioning Organization." *Professional Safety* 50 (11): 34–40.

Liberty Mutual. "A Majority of U.S. Businesses Report Workplace Safety Delivers a Return on Investment." Accessed November 10, 2016, http://www.foysafety.com/safety_news/Liberty%20Mutual%20Survey.pdf.

Lindeman, E. 1961. *The Meaning of Adult Education.* Norman, OK: Harvest House.

Medina, J. 2008. *Brain Rules.* Seattle, WA: Pear Press.

Morrison, K. 2016. "Facing time: Will Criminal Prosecutions under the OSH Act Become More Common?" *Safety & Health* (May): 48–51.

National Safety Council. "Preparing the Business Case for Investment in Safety: A Guide for Safety Practitioners." Accessed April 24, 2017, http://www.nsc.org/MembershipDocuments/JSE-BusCase.pdf.

Oregon OSHA. 2011a. *The Foundation of a Safe Workplace.*

———. 2011b. *Quick guide to safety committees and safety meetings.*

OSHA. 2002. "Job Hazard Analysis." http://www.osha.gov/Publications/osha3071.pdf.

———. "Business Case for Safety and Health." Accessed April 24, 2017, https://www.osha.gov/dcsp/products/topics/businesscase/costs.html.

———. "Safety and Health Add Value." Accessed April 24, 2017, https://www.osha.gov/Publications/safety-health-addvalue.html.

Petersen, D. 2004. "Leadership & Safety Excellence: A Positive Culture Drives Performance. *Professional Safety* 49 (10): 28–32.

Petersen, D., and K. Dotson. 2007. "Executive Safety Leadership." *Professional Safety.* Accessed October 3, 2008, http://www.asse.org/professionalsafety/pastissues/052/05/web0506AS.doc.

Safety & Health. 2015. "DOL & DOJ Agreement: 'New World of Worker Safety.'" http://www.safetyandhealthmagazine.com/articles/13461-dol-doj-agreement-new-world-of-worker-safety.

Senge, P. 2006. *The Fifth Discipline.* New York: Currency Doubleday.

Simon, S., and P. Frazee. 2005. "Building a Better Safety Vehicle: Leadership-driven Culture at General Motors." *Professional Safety* 50 (2): 36–44.

US Department of Justice. 2015. "Memorandum for all United States attorneys." https://www.justice.gov/enrd/file/800431/download.

———. 2016. "Worker Endangerment Initiative." https://www.justice.gov/enrd/worker-endangerment.

Wheatley, M. 2006. *Leadership and the New Science: Discovering Order in a Chaotic World.* San Francisco: Berrett-Koehler, 2006.

Additional Resources

STANDARDS

- ISO 45001—Occupational Health and Safety Management Systems
- OHSAS 18001—Occupational Health and Safety Management Systems
- ANSI/ASSE Z10—Occupational Health and Safety Management Systems
- ANSI/ASSE Z590.3—Prevention through Design: Guidelines for Addressing Occupational Hazards and Risks in Design and Redesign Phases

BOOKS

Friend, M., and J. Kohn. 2014. *Fundamentals of Occupational Safety and Health*, 6th ed. Lanham, MD: Berman Press.

Manuele, F. 2008. *Advanced Safety Management.* Hoboken, NJ: Wiley.

Petersen, D. 2001. *Safety Management: A Human Approach.* Des Plaines, IL: American Society of Safety Engineers.

Phillips, J., P. Phillips, and A. Pulliam. 2014. *Measuring Return on Investment in Environment, Health, and Safety.* Beverly, MA: Scrivener.

WEBSITES

- www.osha.gov—Occupational Safety and Health Administration
- https://www.osha.gov/shpguidelines/—OSHA Recommended Practices for Safety and Health Programs
- www.asse.org—American Society of Safety Engineers
- www.oshrisk.org—Risk Assessment Institute
- www.cdc.gov/niosh—National Institute for Occupational Safety and Health

Acknowledgments

I would like to thank Hal Blythe, who provided initial feedback on the early content and concept of this book. His comments were the pivotal first step in arriving at the point where the book exists today. I would also like to thank the peer-review committee who spent a great amount of time reading and providing feedback on the initial draft. It is a "big ask" to request seasoned veterans to take time out of their schedule to read through a book draft and provide their expert feedback. The peer-review panel encompassed a variety of disciplines, including occupational safety, human resources, plant operations, workers' compensation, and academia. Its members are Lori Beers, Paul English, Matt Gibbons, Bob Nickel, Linda Reynolds, Shawn Reynolds, Judy Spain, Norm Spain, and Lisa Terry.

I would like to thank Suzanne and Sue at CreateSpace for their outstanding work in editing my manuscript. Any errors that remain are mine. I would also like to thank the CreateSpace production team for all of their work in bringing an ambitious idea to a finished product. You have made this an exceptional experience.

About the Author

E. Scott Dunlap holds a doctoral degree in higher and adult education from the University of Memphis and is a board-certified safety professional. He worked as a safety professional in government and industry for more than fourteen years before he went on to teach in the graduate safety, security, and emergency management program at Eastern Kentucky University.

Throughout his career, he improved safety performance for organizations such as Nike, Cargill, Archer Daniels Midland, and AutoZone.

Dr. Dunlap has spoken at regional and national conferences on occupational safety issues. He is the author of twelve articles, three books, and one book chapter on occupational safety issues.

www.ingramcontent.com/pod-product-compliance
Lightning Source LLC
Chambersburg PA
CBHW070027210526
45170CB00012B/213